Illustrations for Preaching and Teaching

Illustrations for Preaching and Teaching

From *Leadership Journal*

Edited by
Craig Brian Larson

BakerBooks
A Division of Baker Book House Co
Grand Rapids, Michigan 49516

Illustrations for Preaching and Teaching:
From *Leadership Journal*

Co-published by Christianity Today, Inc., and Baker Book House Company. Distributed by Baker Book House Company.

Fourth printing, March 1995

Printed in the United States of America

Library of Congress Cataloging-in-Publication Data

Illustrations for preaching and teaching : from Leadership journal / edited by Craig Brian Larson.
p. cm.
Includes bibliographical references.
ISBN 0-8010-5691-8
1. Homiletical illustrations. I. Larson, Craig Brian.
II. Leadership (Carol Stream, Ill.)
BV4225.2.I456 1993
251'.08—dc20 93-23484

Introduction

Preachers crave illustrations like the thundering steam locomotives of yesteryear did coal. Whether we preach one sermon a week or three, whether we're veterans in the pulpit or novices, we burn illustrations as fast as they're shoveled in.

Unlike coal, however, a telling illustration is as rare and valuable as a diamond. Out of the scores of illustrations submitted each quarter for To Illustrate, the column of sermon illustrations in LEADERSHIP, only eight to twelve glitter bright enough for publication.

As editors of LEADERSHIP, we have often had readers tell us, "When a new issue comes in the mail, the first thing I read (after the cartoons) is To Illustrate. Then I have my secretary copy and file the illustrations."

Recognizing their enduring value, we decided to compile the best of LEADERSHIP's To Illustrate under one cover. As we discussed the design of this book, we felt three characteristics would make it most useful for pastors:

1. *The right to copy.* The publisher grants you the right to copy the illustrations. So you can file them in the way that works best for your system.

2. *Alternate subjects and index.* Each illustration is followed by two alternate subjects in parentheses. Since any good illustration can illustrate several different subjects with slight modification, you can copy and file each illustration under three categories if you like. Each illustration is indexed under all three titles.

3. *Complete illustrations on a single page.* Typically the illustrations don't run from page to page. Each is contained on one page, making it easier to copy and use in the pulpit.

In an interview, popular preacher Steve Brown once said, "At seminary your homiletics professor said, 'It is beneath a man of God to use an illustration book.' He's lying, folks, he's lying through his teeth. If you get one good illustration out of an illustration book, it's worth every dime you paid for it. . . . If we don't illustrate, we ought not teach."

Preach it, Steve!

We're confident readers will find more than one diamond in this book, enabling them to communicate the gospel message with imagination and impact.

— *Craig Brian Larson*
associate editor, LEADERSHIP
Carol Stream, Illinois

Adversity 1

Farmers in southern Alabama were accustomed to planting one crop every year—cotton. They would plow as much ground as they could and plant their crop. Year after year they lived by cotton.

Then one year the dreaded boll weevil devastated the whole area. So the next year the farmers mortgaged their homes and planted cotton again, hoping for a good harvest. But as the cotton began to grow, the insect came back and destroyed the crop, wiping out most of the farms.

The few who survived those two years of the boll weevil decided to experiment the third year, so they planted something they'd never planted before—peanuts. And peanuts proved so hardy and the market proved so ravenous for that product that the farmers who survived the first two years reaped profits that third year that enabled them to pay off all their debts. They planted peanuts from then on and prospered greatly.

Then you know what those farmers did? They spent some of their new wealth to erect in the town square a monument—to the boll weevil. If it hadn't been for the boll weevil, they never would have discovered peanuts. They learned that even out of disaster there can be great delight.

(Change, God's goodness)

Apathy 2

In *Youthworker Journal,* Will Eisenhower recalls one night as a counselor at a Bible camp:

It had been an exhausting day; the guys in my cabin were asleep; and I was dead to the world. Then there came a dim awareness: Ants were crawling all over my body. I was so tired, and sleep felt so good, that I actually resisted rousing myself. I knew that if I were roused even a little bit, I would have to acknowledge that my sleeping bag had become an ant freeway. I didn't want to know the awful truth, so for at least several seconds I tried to fight it. At some deep level, I told myself that sleep was the reality and the ants were a dream.

Apathy is sort of like sleeping through an ant attack. Waking up means I have to recognize that although foxes have safe places to hide, the Son of Man doesn't, and his followers don't either. This world is fundamentally opposed to me, and wants to attack me when I am least prepared for it. No wonder some of us would rather stay asleep.

(Watchfulness, World)

Assumptions 3

A traveler, between flights at an airport, went to a lounge and bought a small package of cookies. Then she sat down and began reading a newspaper. Gradually, she became aware of a rustling noise. From behind her paper, she was flabbergasted to see a neatly dressed man helping himself to her cookies. Not wanting to make a scene, she leaned over and took a cookie herself.

A minute or two passed, and then came more rustling. He was helping himself to another cookie! By this time, they had come to the end of the package, but she was so angry she didn't dare allow herself to say anything. Then, as if to add insult to injury, the man broke the remaining cookie in two, pushed half across to her, and ate the other half and left.

Still fuming some time later when her flight was announced, the woman opened her handbag to get her ticket. To her shock and embarrassment, there she found her pack of unopened cookies!

How wrong our assumptions can be.

(Misunderstandings, Kindness)

Atonement 4

Ron Rand writes in *For Fathers Who Aren't in Heaven:*

Michael usually takes his family out each week to see a movie or sports event. When they come home, they make a fire in the fireplace and pop popcorn.

During one of these evenings, little Billy made a real pest of himself in the car on the drive home, so he was punished by being sent to sit in his bedroom while the rest of the family had popcorn. After the family had the fire going and the popcorn ready, Michael went back to Billy's room and said, "You go out with the others. I'll stay here and take your punishment."

Through Michael's action, the entire family experienced a vivid example of what Jesus did for everyone.

(Love, Fathers)

Atonement 5

One winter's night in 1935, it is told, Fiorello LaGuardia, the irrepressible mayor of New York, showed up at a night court in the poorest ward of the city. He dismissed the judge for the evening and took over the bench. That night a tattered old woman, charged with stealing a loaf of bread, was brought before him. She defended herself by saying, "My daughter's husband has deserted her. She is sick, and her children are starving."

The shopkeeper refused to drop the charges, saying, "It's a bad neighborhood, your honor, and she's got to be punished to teach other people a lesson."

LaGuardia sighed. He turned to the old woman and said, "I've got to punish you; the law makes no exceptions. Ten dollars or ten days in jail." However, even while pronouncing sentence, La Guardia reached into his pocket, took out a ten-dollar bill, and threw it into his hat with these famous words: "Here's the ten-dollar fine, which I now remit, and furthermore, I'm going to fine everyone in the courtroom fifty cents for living in a town where a person has to steal bread so that her grandchildren can eat. Mr. Bailiff, collect the fines and give them to the defendant."

The following day, a New York newspaper reported: "Forty-seven dollars and fifty cents was turned over to a bewildered old grandmother who had stolen a loaf of bread to feed her starving grandchildren. Making forced donations were a red-faced storekeeper, seventy petty criminals, and a few New York policemen."

(Law, Mercy)

Attitude 6

The March 1988 *Rotarian* tells the story of a certain organization offering a bounty of $5,000 for wolves captured alive. It turned Sam and Jed into fortune hunters. Day and night they scoured the mountains and forests looking for their valuable prey.

Exhausted one night, they fell asleep dreaming of their potential fortune. Suddenly, Sam awoke to see that they were surrounded by about fifty wolves with flaming eyes and bared teeth. He nudged his friend and said, "Jed, wake up! We're rich!"

(Faith, Trials)

Beginnings 7

On a plaque marking Abraham Lincoln's birthplace near Hodgenville, Kentucky, is recorded this scrap of conversation:

"Any news down t' the village, Ezry?"

"Well, Squire McLains's gone t' Washington t' see Madison swore in, and ol' Spellman tells me this Bonaparte fella has captured most o' Spain. What's new out here, neighbor?"

"Nuthin', nuthin' a'tall, 'cept fer a new baby born t' Tom Lincoln's. Nothin' ever happens out here."

Some events, whether birthdays in Hodgenville (or Bethlehem) or spiritual rebirth in a person's life, may not create much earthly splash, but those of lasting importance will eventually get the notice they deserve.

(Children, News)

Belief 8

Robert Chesebrough believed in his product. He's the fellow who invented Vaseline, a petroleum jelly refined from rod wax, the ooze that forms on shafts of oil rigs. He so believed in the healing properties of his product that he became his own guinea pig. He burned himself with acid and flame; he cut and scratched himself so often and so deeply that he bore the scars of his tests the rest of his life. But he proved his product worked. People had only to look at his wounds, now healed, to see the value of his work—and the extent of his belief.

(Commitment, Evidence)

Belief 9

Actor Cary Grant once told how he was walking along a street and met a fellow whose eyes locked onto him with excitement. The man said, "Wait a minute, you're . . . you're—I know who you are; don't tell me—uh, Rock Hud . . . No, you're . . ."

Grant thought he'd help him, so he finished the man's sentence: "Cary Grant."

And the fellow said, "No, that's not it! You're . . ."

There was Cary Grant identifying himself with his own name, but the fellow had someone else in mind.

John says of Jesus, "He was in the world, and though the world was made through him, the world did not recognize him" (John 1:10). And even when Jesus identified who he was—the Son of God—the response was not a welcome recognition, but rather the Crucifixion.

(Spiritual perception, Christ)

Blame 10

John Killinger tells about the manager of a minor league baseball team who was so disgusted with his center fielder's performance that he ordered him to the dugout and assumed the position himself. The first ball that came into center field took a bad hop and hit the manager in the mouth. The next one was a high fly ball, which he lost in the glare of the sun—until it bounced off his forehead. The third was a hard line drive that he charged with outstretched arms; unfortunately, it flew between his hands and smacked his eye.

Furious, he ran back to the dugout, grabbed the center fielder by the uniform, and shouted, "You idiot! You've got center field so messed up that even I can't do a thing with it!"

(Failure, Judging others)

Blood of Christ 11

Dennis Fulton, former pilot with the Wings of Caring ministry in Zaire, tells of landing a newly purchased Cessna 402 at one of his regular stops in the back country.

As always, the villagers excitedly gathered around the plane, but this time Dennis was approached by two men carrying a live chicken. One had the bird by the feet, and the other had it by the head, and before either the chicken or Dennis knew what was happening, the fowl's head and body parted company. The man with the flopping chicken corpse began swinging it over his head, round and round, with predictable results. Dressed in a freshly pressed white shirt, Dennis was splattered with chicken blood, as were the plane and the villagers.

When Dennis asked what that meant, a native explained that for generations, the splattered blood had signified an end to suffering. To the people of Zaire, the Cessna promised hope and help of all kinds.

In a graphic way, the splattered blood of that chicken, signifying the end of suffering, was a fitting reminder of the blood Christ shed to end the suffering of a world caught in the grip of sin.

(Christ, Suffering)

Body of Christ 12

In March of 1981, President Ronald Reagan was shot by John Hinckley, Jr., and was hospitalized for several weeks. Although Reagan was the nation's chief executive, his hospitalization had little impact on the nation's activity. Government continued on.

On the other hand, suppose the garbage collectors in this country went on strike, as they did in Philadelphia. That city was not only in a literal mess, the pile of decaying trash quickly became a health hazard. A three week nationwide strike would paralyze the country.

Who is more important—the President or a garbage collector?

In the body of Christ, seemingly insignificant ones are urgently needed. As Paul reminds us, "The head cannot say to the feet, 'I don't need you!' On the contrary, those parts of the body that seem to be weaker are indispensable" (1 Cor. 12:21-22).

(Spiritual gifts, Servanthood)

Burdens 13

In the Philippines the driver of a carabao wagon was on his way to market when he overtook an old man carrying a heavy load. Taking compassion on him, the driver invited the old man to ride in the wagon. Gratefully the old man accepted.

After a few minutes, the driver turned to see how the man was doing. To his surprise, he found him still straining under the heavy weight, for he had not taken the burden off his shoulders.

Christ offers rest to all who will trust him completely.

(Rest, Trust)

Caring 14

From 1986 to 1990, Frank Reed was held hostage in a Lebanon cell. For months at a time Reed was blindfolded, living in complete darkness, or chained to a wall and kept in absolute silence. On one occasion, he was moved to another room, and, although blindfolded, he could sense others in the room. Yet it was three weeks before he dared peek out to discover he was chained next to Terry Anderson and Tom Sutherland.

Although he was beaten, made ill, and tormented, Reed felt most the lack of anyone caring. He said in an interview with *Time,* "Nothing I did mattered to anyone. I began to realize how withering it is to exist with not a single expression of caring around [me]. . . . I learned one overriding fact: caring is a powerful force. If no one cares, you are truly alone."

Christians, who are never truly alone, are also fortunate to receive God's gracious care through the church. This care can provide the strength to endure.

(Church, Loneliness)

Change 15

For years, the opening of "The Wide World of Sports" television program illustrated "the agony of defeat" with a painful ending to an attempted ski jump. The skier appeared in good form as he headed down the jump, but then, for no apparent reason, he tumbled head over heels off the side of the jump, bouncing off the supporting structure.

What viewers didn't know was that he chose to fall rather than finish the jump. Why? As he explained later, the jump surface had become too fast, and midway down the ramp, he realized if he completed the jump, he would land on the level ground, beyond the safe sloping landing area, which could have been fatal.

As it was, the skier suffered no more than a headache from the tumble.

To change one's course in life can be a dramatic and sometimes painful undertaking, but change is better than a fatal landing at the end.

(Failure, Decisions)

Character **16**

The Scriptures often exhort us to be filled with various godly virtues—which means what? How do we know if we are "full of goodness" (Rom. 15:14), for example?

Think a moment about a water-saturated sponge. If we push down with our finger even slightly, water runs out onto the table. We immediately know what fills the interior pockets of the sponge.

The same is true of ourselves. We can tell what fills us on the inside by what comes out under pressure.

(Pressure, Tests)

Character 17

Carl Lundquist in *Silent Issues of the Church,* writes:

Henry Wingblade used to say that Christian personality is hidden deep inside us. It is unseen, like the soup carried in a tureen high over a waiter's head. No one knows what's inside —unless the waiter is bumped and he trips!

Just so, people don't know what's inside us until we've been bumped. But if Christ is living inside, what spills out is the fruit of the Spirit.

(Fruits of the Spirit, Trials)

Christ 18

Em Griffin writes, in *Making Friends,* about three kinds of London maps: the street map, the map depicting throughways, and the underground map of the subway. "Each map is accurate and correct," he writes, "but each map does not give the complete picture. To see the whole, the three maps must be printed one on top of each other. However, that is often confusing, so I use only one 'layer' at a time.

"It is the same with the words used to describe the death of Jesus Christ. Each word, like *redemption, reconciliation,* or *justification,* is accurate and correct, but each word does not give the complete picture. To see the whole we need to place one 'layer' on top of the other, but that is sometimes confusing—we cannot see the trees for the whole! So we separate out each splendid concept and discover that the whole is more than the sum of its parts."

(Theology, Christ's death)

Christ's death 19

In his book *Written in Blood,* Robert Coleman tells the story of a little boy whose sister needed a blood transfusion. The doctor had explained that she had the same disease the boy had recovered from two years earlier. Her only chance for recovery was a transfusion from someone who had previously conquered the disease. Since the two children had the same rare blood type, the boy was the ideal donor.

"Would you give your blood to Mary?" the doctor asked.

Johnny hesitated. His lower lip started to tremble. Then he smiled and said, "Sure, for my sister."

Soon the two children were wheeled into the hospital room—Mary, pale and thin; Johnny, robust and healthy. Neither spoke, but when their eyes met, Johnny grinned.

As the nurse inserted the needle into his arm, Johnny's smile faded. He watched the blood flow through the tube. With the ordeal almost over, his voice, slightly shaky, broke the silence. "Doctor, when do I die?"

Only then did the doctor realize why Johnny had hesitated, why his lip had trembled when he'd agreed to donate his blood. He'd thought giving his blood to his sister meant giving up his life. In that brief moment, he'd made his great decision.

Johnny, fortunately, didn't have to die to save his sister. Each of us however, has a condition more serious than Mary's, and it required Jesus to give not just his blood, but his life.

(Love, Sacrifice)

Christ's death **20**

A small boy was consistently late coming home from school. His parents warned him that he must be home on time that afternoon, but nevertheless he arrived later than ever. His mother met him at the door and said nothing. His father met him in the living room and said nothing.

At dinner that night, the boy looked at his plate. There was a slice of bread and a glass of water. He looked at his father's full plate and then at his father, but his father remained silent. The boy was crushed.

The father waited for the full impact to sink in, then quietly took the boy's plate and placed it in front of himself. He took his own plate of meat and potatoes, put it in front of the boy, and smiled at his son.

When that boy grew to be a man, he said, "All my life I've known what God is like by what my father did that night."

(Fathers, Example)

Christ, unchanging 21

When Lloyd C. Douglas, author of *The Robe* and other novels, was a university student, he lived in a boarding house, says Maxie Dunnam in *Jesus' Claims—Our Promises.* Downstairs on the first floor was an elderly, retired music teacher, now infirm and unable to leave the apartment.

Douglas said that every morning they had a ritual they would go through together. He would come down the steps, open the old man's door, and ask, "Well, what's the good news?"

The old man would pick up his tuning fork, tap it on the side of his wheelchair, and say, "That's Middle C! It was middle C yesterday; it will be middle C tomorrow; it will be middle C a thousand years from now. The tenor upstairs sings flat, the piano across the hall is out of tune, but my friend, that is middle C!"

The old man had discovered one thing upon which he could depend, one constant reality in his life, one "still point in a turning world." For Christians, the one "still point in a turning world," the one absolute of which there is no shadow of turning, is Jesus Christ.

(Gospel, Change)

Christian 22

What is a Christian? In the *Letter to Diognetus,* which dates back to the second century B.C., an anonymous writer describes a strange people who are in the world but not of the world:

Christians are not differentiated from other people by country, language, or customs; you see, they do not live in cities of their own, or speak some strange dialect. . . . They live in both Greek and foreign cities, wherever chance has put them. They follow local customs in clothing, food, and the other aspects of life. But at the same time, they demonstrate to us the unusual form of their own citizenship.

They live in their own native lands, but as aliens. . . . Every foreign country is to them as their native country, and every native land as a foreign country.

They marry and have children just like everyone else, but they do not kill unwanted babies. They offer a shared table, but not a shared bed. They are passing their days on earth, but are citizens of heaven. They obey the appointed laws and go beyond the laws in their own lives.

They love everyone, but are persecuted by all. They are put to death and gain life. They are poor and yet make many rich. They are dishonored and yet gain glory through dishonor. Their names are blackened, and yet they are cleared. They are mocked and bless in return. They are treated outrageously and behave respectfully to others.

When they do good, they are punished as evildoers; when punished, they rejoice as if being given new life. They are attacked by Jews as aliens and are persecuted by Greeks; yet those who hate them cannot give any reason for their hostility.

(Persecution, Separation)

Church 23

Power can be used in at least two ways: it can be unleashed, or it can be harnessed.

The energy in ten gallons of gasoline, for instance, can be released explosively by dropping a lighted match into the can. Or it can be channeled through a car engine in a controlled burn and used to transport a person 350 miles.

Explosions are spectacular, but controlled burns have lasting effect, staying power.

The Holy Spirit works both ways. At Pentecost, he exploded on the scene; his presence was like "tongues of fire" (Acts 2:3). Thousands were affected by one burst of God's power. But he also works through the church—the institution God began to tap the Holy Spirit's power for the long haul. Through worship, fellowship, and service, Christians are provided with staying power.

(Power, Holy Spirit)

Church 24

Gregory Elder writes:

Growing up on the Atlantic Coast, I spent long hours working on intricate sand castles; whole cities would appear beneath my hands.

One year, for several days in a row, I was accosted by bullies who smashed my creations. Finally I tried an experiment: I placed cinder blocks, rocks, and chunks of concrete in the base of my castles. Then I built the sand kingdoms on top of the rocks.

When the local toughs appeared (and I disappeared), their bare feet suddenly met their match.

Many people see the church in grave peril from a variety of dangers: secularism, politics, heresies, or plain old sin. They forget that the church is built upon a Rock (Matt. 16:16), over which the gates of hell itself shall not prevail.

(World, Faith)

Church 25

When it was built for an international exposition in the last century, the structure was called monstrous by the citizens of the city, who demanded it be torn down as soon as the exposition was over.

Yet from the moment its architect first conceived it, he took pride in it and loyally defended it from those who wished to destroy it. He knew it was destined for greatness. Today it is one of the architectural wonders of the modern world and stands as the primary landmark of Paris, France. The architect, of course, was Alexandre Gustave Eiffel. His famous tower was built in 1889.

In the same way we are struck by Jesus' loyalty to another structure—the church—which he entrusted to an unlikely band of disciples, whom he defended, prayed for, and prepared to spread the gospel. To outsiders they (and we) must seem like incapable blunderers. But Jesus, the architect of the church, knows this structure is destined for greatness when he returns.

(Creator, Critics)

Church 26

The article "What Good Is a Tree?" in *Reader's Digest* explained that when the roots of trees touch, there is a substance present that reduces competition. In fact, this unknown fungus helps link roots of different trees—even of dissimilar species. A whole forest may be linked together. If one tree has access to water, another to nutrients, and a third to sunlight, the trees have the means to share with one another.

Like trees in a forest, Christians in the church need and support one another.

(Unity, Support)

Church 27

In *Witnesses of a Third Way: A Fresh Look at Evangelism,* Robert Neff's chapter includes this story about visiting a church service:

It was one of those mornings when the tenor didn't get out of bed on the right side. . . . As I listened to his faltering voice, I looked around. People were pulling out hymnals to locate the hymn being sung by the soloist. By the second verse, the congregation had joined the soloist in the hymn. By the third verse, the tenor was beginning to find the range. By the fourth verse, it was beautiful. And on the fifth verse the congregation was absolutely silent, and the tenor sang the most beautiful solo of his life.

That is life in the body of Christ, enabling one another to sing the tune Christ has given us.

(Support, Spiritual gifts)

Church attendance 28

Not long ago, the world watched as three gray whales, icebound off Point Barrow, Alaska, floated battered and bloody, gasping for breath at a hole in the ice. Their only hope: somehow to be transported five miles past the ice pack to open sea.

Rescuers began cutting a string of breathing holes about twenty yards apart in the six-inch-thick ice. For eight days they coaxed the whales from one hole to the next, mile after mile. Along the way, one of the trio vanished and was presumed dead. But finally, with the help of Russian icebreakers, the whales Putu and Siku swam to freedom.

In a way, worship is a string of breathing holes the Lord provides his people. Battered and bruised in a world frozen over with greed, selfishness, and hatred, we rise for air in church, a place to breathe again, to be loved and encouraged, until that day when the Lord forever shatters the ice cap.

(Worship, Encouragement)

Ten Commandments 29

In *To My People With Love,* John Killinger writes:

In her beautiful novel about Maine, *The Country of the Pointed Firs,* Sara Orne Jewett describes the ascent of a woman writer on the pathway leading to the home of a retired sea captain named Elijah Tilley. On the way, the woman notes a number of wooden stakes randomly scattered about the property, with no discernible order. Each is painted white and trimmed in yellow, like the captain's house.

Curious, she asks Captain Tilley what they mean. When he first plowed the ground, he says, his plow snagged on many large rocks just beneath the surface. So he set out stakes where the rocks lay in order to avoid them in the future.

In a sense, this is what God has done with the Ten Commandments. . . . He has said, "These are the trouble spots in life. Avoid these, and you won't snag your plow."

(Warnings, Commandments)

Commitment 30

Tim Bowden, in his book *One Crowded Hour* about cameraman Neil Davis, tells about an incident that happened in Borneo during the confrontation between Malaysia and Indonesia in 1964.

A group of Gurkhas from Nepal were asked if they would be willing to jump from transport planes into combat against the Indonesians if the need arose. The Gurkhas had the right to turn down the request because they had never been trained as paratroopers. Bowden quotes Davis's account of the story:

"Now the Gurkhas usually agreed to anything, but on this occasion they provisionally rejected the plan. But the next day one of their NCOs sought out the British officer who made the request and said they had discussed the matter further and would be prepared to jump under certain conditions.

" 'What are they?' asked the British officer.

"The Gurkhas told him they would jump if the land was marshy or reasonably soft with no rocky outcrops, because they were inexperienced in falling. The British officer considered this, and said that the dropping area would almost certainly be over jungle, and there would not be rocky outcrops, so that seemed all right. Was there anything else?

"Yes, said the Gurkhas. They wanted the plane to fly as slowly as possible and no more than one hundred feet high. The British officer pointed out the planes always did fly as slowly as possible when dropping troops, but to jump from 100 feet was impossible, because the parachutes would not open in time from that height.

" 'Oh,' said the Gurkhas, 'that's all right, then. We'll jump with parachutes anywhere. You didn't mention parachutes before!' "

Any church could use such Gurkha-like commitment and courage.

(Courage, Service)

Commitment 31

One Haitian pastor illustrates the need for total commitment to Christ with this parable:

A certain man wanted to sell his house for $2,000. Another man wanted very badly to buy it, but because he was poor, he couldn't afford the full price. After much bargaining, the owner agreed to sell the house for half the original price with just one stipulation: he would retain ownership of one small nail protruding from just over the door.

After several years, the original owner wanted the house back, but the new owner was unwilling to sell. So first the owner went out, found the carcass of a dead dog, and hung it from the nail he still owned. Soon the house became unlivable, and the family was forced to sell the house to the owner of the nail.

The Haitian pastor's conclusion: "If we leave the Devil with even one small peg in our life, he will return to hang his rotting garbage on it, making it unfit for Christ's habitation."

(Consecration, Satan)

Complacency 32

Ronald Meredith, in his book *Hurryin' Big for Little Reasons,* describes one quiet night in early spring:

Suddenly out of the night came the sound of wild geese flying. I ran to the house and breathlessly announced the excitement I felt. What is to compare with wild geese across the moon?

It might have ended there except for the sight of our tame mallards on the pond. They heard the wild call they had once known. The honking out of the night sent little arrows of prompting deep into their wild yesterdays. Their wings fluttered a feeble response. The urge to fly—to take their place in the sky for which God made them—was sounding in their feathered breasts, but they never raised from the water.

The matter had been settled long ago. The corn of the barnyard was too tempting! Now their desire to fly only made them uncomfortable. Temptation is always enjoyed at the price of losing the capacity for flight.

(Temptation, Call of God)

Conscience 33

In *Focus on the Family,* Rolf Zettersten writes:

A good friend in North Carolina bought a new car with a voice-warning system. . . . At first Edwin was amused to hear the soft female voice gently remind him that his seat belt wasn't fastened. . . . Edwin affectionately called this voice the "little woman."

He soon discovered his little woman was programmed to warn him about his gasoline. "Your fuel level is low," she said one time in her sweet voice. Edwin nodded his head and thanked her. He figured he still had enough to go another fifty miles, so he kept on driving. But a few minutes later, her voice interrupted again with the same warning. And so it went over and over. Although he knew it was the same recording, Edwin thought her voice sounded harsher each time.

Finally, he stopped his car and crawled under the dashboard. After a quick search, he found the appropriate wires and gave them a good yank. So much for the little woman.

He was still smiling to himself a few miles later when his car began sputtering and coughing. He ran out of gas! Somewhere inside the dashboard, Edwin was sure he could hear the little woman laughing.

People like Edwin learn before long that the little voice inside, although ignored or even disconnected, often tells them exactly what they need to know.

(Disobedience, Word of God)

Conversion 34

Living without Christ is like driving a car with its front end out of line. You can stay on the road if you grip the steering wheel with both hands and hang on tightly. Any lapse of attention, however, and you head straight for the ditch.

Society in general—educators, political leaders, parents—exhorts us to drive straight and curb our destructive tendencies. But it is a ceaseless struggle.

Coming to Christ is a little like getting a front-end alignment. The pull toward the ditch is corrected from the inside.

Not to say there won't be bumps and potholes ahead that will still try to jar us off the road. Temptations and challenges will always test our alertness to steer a straight course. We can hardly afford to fall asleep at the wheel. But the basic skew in the moral mechanism has been repaired.

(Regeneration, Obedience)

Cooperation 35

CBS radio newsman Charles Osgood told the story of two ladies who lived in a convalescent center. Each had suffered an incapacitating stroke. Margaret's stroke left her left side restricted, while Ruth's stroke damaged her right side. Both of these ladies were accomplished pianists but had given up hope of ever playing again.

The director of the center sat them down at a piano and encouraged them to play solo pieces together. They did, and a beautiful friendship developed.

What a picture of the church's needing to work together! What one member cannot do alone, perhaps two or more could do together—in harmony.

(Spiritual gifts, Church)

Courage 36

Peter Cartwright, a nineteenth-century, circuit riding, Methodist preacher, was an uncompromising man. One Sunday morning when he was to preach, he was told that President Andrew Jackson was in the congregation, and was warned not to say anything out of line.

When Cartwright stood to preach, he said, "I understand that Andrew Jackson is here. I have been requested to be guarded in my remarks. Andrew Jackson will go to hell if he doesn't repent."

The congregation was shocked and wondered how the President would respond. After the service, President Jackson shook hands with Peter Cartwright and said, "Sir, if I had a regiment of men like you, I could whip the world."

(Preaching, Hell)

Courage 37

Charles Colson, in *Loving God,* tells the story of Telemachus, a fourth-century Christian.

He lived in a remote village, tending his garden and spending much of his time in prayer. One day he thought he heard the voice of God telling him to go to Rome, so he obeyed, setting out on foot. Weary weeks later, he arrived in the city at the time of a great festival. The little monk followed the crowd surging down the streets into the Colosseum. He saw the gladiators stand before the emperor and say, "We who are about to die salute you." Then he realized these men were going to fight to the death for the entertainment of the crowd. He cried out, "In the name of Christ, stop!"

As the games began, he pushed his way through the crowd, climbed over the wall, and dropped to the floor of the arena. When the crowd saw this tiny figure rushing to the gladiators and saying, "In the name of Christ, stop!" they thought it was part of the show and began laughing.

When they realized it wasn't, the laughter turned to anger. As he was pleading with the gladiators to stop, one of them plunged a sword into his body. He fell to the sand. As he was dying, his last words were, "In the name of Christ, stop!"

Then a strange thing happened. The gladiators stood looking at the tiny figure lying there. A hush fell over the Colosseum. Way up in the upper rows, a man stood and made his way to the exit. Others began to follow. In dead silence, everyone left the Colosseum.

The year was B.C. 391, and that was the last battle to the death between gladiators in the Roman Colosseum. Never again in the great stadium did men kill each other for the entertainment of the crowd, all because of one tiny voice that could hardly be heard above the tumult. One voice—one life—that spoke the truth in God's name.

(Sacrifice, Testimony)

Covenant 38

Bruce Shelley in *Christian Theology in Plain Language,* writes:

In modern times we define a host of relations by contracts. These are usually for goods or services and for hard cash. The contract, formal or informal, helps to specify failure in these relationships.

The Lord did not establish a contract with Israel or with the church. He created a covenant. There is a difference.

Contracts are broken when one of the parties fails to keep his promise. If, let us say, a patient fails to keep an appointment with a doctor, the doctor is not obligated to call the house and inquire, "Where were you? Why didn't you show up for your appointment?" He simply goes on to his next patient and has his appointment-secretary take note of the patient who failed to keep the appointment. The patient may find it harder the next time to see the doctor. He broke an informal contract.

According to the Bible, however, the Lord asks: "Can a mother forget the baby at her breast and have no compassion on the child she has borne? Though she may forget, I will not forget you!" (Isa. 49:15).

The Bible indicates the covenant is more like the ties of a parent to her child than it is a doctor's appointment. If a child fails to show up for dinner, the parent's obligation, unlike the doctor's, isn't canceled. The parent finds out where the child is and makes sure he's cared for. One member's failure does not destroy the relationship. A covenant puts no conditions on faithfulness. It is the unconditional commitment to love and serve.

(Faithfulness, God's love)

Creation 39

In the town hall in Copenhagen stands the world's most complicated clock. It took forty years to build at a cost of more than a million dollars. That clock has ten faces, fifteen thousand parts, and is accurate to two-fifths of a second every three hundred years. The clock computes the time of day, the days of the week, the months and years, and the movements of the planets for twenty-five hundred years. Some parts of that clock will not move until twenty-five centuries have passed.

What is intriguing about that clock is that it is not accurate. It loses two-fifths of a second every three hundred years. Like all clocks, that timepiece in Copenhagen must be regulated by a more precise clock, the universe itself. That mighty astronomical clock with its billions of moving parts, from atoms to stars, rolls on century after century with movements so reliable that all time on earth can be measured against it.

(Time, God's sovereignty)

Criticism **40**

A young musician's concert was poorly received by the critics. The famous Finish composer Jean Sibelius consoled him by patting him on the shoulder and saying, "Remember, son, there is no city in the world where they have erected a statue to a critic."

(Persistence, Reputation)

Cross 41

The Viet Nam Veteran's Memorial is striking for its simplicity. Etched in a black granite wall are the names of 58,156 Americans who died in that war.

Since its opening in 1982, the stark monument has stirred deep emotions. Some visitors walk its length slowly, reverently, and without pause. Others stop before certain names, remembering their son or sweetheart or fellow soldier, wiping away tears, tracing the names with their fingers.

For three Viet Nam veterans—Robert Bedker, Willard Craig, and Darrall Lausch—a visit to the memorial must be especially poignant, for they can walk up to the long ebony wall and find their own names carved in the stone. Because of data-coding errors, each of them was incorrectly listed as killed in action.

Dead, but alive—a perfect description of the Christian.

(Death, Christian)

Cross 42

In *Planet in Rebellion,* George Vandeman writes:

It was May 21, 1946. The place: Los Alamos. A young and daring scientist was carrying out a necessary experiment in preparation for the atomic test to be conducted in the waters of the South Pacific atoll at Bikini.

He had successfully performed such an experiment many times before. In his effort to determine the amount of U-235 necessary for a chain reaction—scientists call it the critical mass—he would push two hemispheres of uranium together. Then, just as the mass became critical, he would push them apart with his screwdriver, thus instantly stopping the chain reaction.

But that day, just as the material became critical, the screwdriver slipped. The hemispheres of uranium came too close together. Instantly the room was filled with a dazzling bluish haze. Young Louis Slotin, instead of ducking and thereby possibly saving himself, tore the two hemispheres apart with his hands and thus interrupted the chain reaction.

By this instant, self-forgetful daring, he saved the lives of the seven other persons in the room. . . . As he waited for the car that was to take them to the hospital, he said quietly to his companion, "You'll come through all right. But I haven't the faintest chance myself." It was only too true. Nine days later he died in agony.

Nineteen centuries ago the Son of the living God walked directly into sin's most concentrated radiation, allowed himself to be touched by its curse, and let it take his life. . . . But by that act he broke the chain reaction. He broke the power of sin.

(Sacrifice, Sin)

Cross 43

Clarence Jordan, author of the *Cotton Patch* New Testament translation and founder of the interracial Koinonia farm in Americus, Georgia, was getting a red-carpet tour of another minister's church. With pride the minister pointed to the rich, imported pews and luxurious decorations.

As they stepped outside, darkness was falling, and a spotlight shone on a huge cross atop the steeple.

"That cross alone cost us ten thousand dollars," the minister said with a satisfied smile.

"You got cheated," said Jordan. "Times were when Christians could get them for free."

(Impressions, Money)

Crucifixion 44

C. Truman Davis, M.D., in *The Expositer's Bible Commentary* writes:

What is crucifixion? A medical doctor provides a physical description: The cross is placed on the ground and the exhausted man is quickly thrown backwards with his shoulders against the wood. The legionnaire feels for the depression at the front of the wrist. He drives a heavy, square wrought-iron nail through the wrist and deep into the wood. Quickly he moves to the other side and repeats the action, being careful not to pull the arms too tightly, but to allow some flex and movement. The cross is then lifted into place.

The left foot is pressed backward against the right foot, and with both feet extended, toes down, a nail is driven through the arch of each, leaving the knees flexed. The victim is now crucified. As he slowly sags down with more weight on the nails in the wrists, excruciating, fiery pain shoots along the fingers and up the arms to explode in the brain—the nails in the wrists are putting pressure on the median nerves. As he pushes himself upward to avoid stretching torment, he places the full weight on the nail through his feet. Again he feels the searing agony of the nail tearing through the nerves between the bones of the feet.

As the arms fatigue, cramps sweep through the muscles, knotting them in deep, relentless, throbbing pain. With these cramps comes the inability to push himself upward to breathe. Air can be drawn into the lungs but not exhaled. He fights to raise himself in order to get even one small breath. Finally carbon dioxide builds up in the lungs and in the blood stream, and the cramps partially subside. Spasmodically he is able to push himself upward to exhale and bring in life-giving oxygen.

Hours of this limitless pain, cycles of twisting, joint-rending cramps, intermittent partial asphyxiation, searing pain as tissue is torn from his lacerated back as he moves up and down against the rough timber. Then another agony begins: a deep, crushing pain deep in the chest as the pericardium slowly fills with serum and begins to compress the heart.

It is now almost over—the loss of tissue fluids reached a critical level—the compressed heart is struggling to pump heavy, thick, sluggish blood into the tissues—the tortured lungs are making a frantic effort to gasp in small gulps of air.

He can feel the chill of death creeping through his tissues. . . . Finally he can allow his body to die.

All this the Bible records with the simple words, "And they crucified him" (Mark 15:24).

What wondrous love is this?

(Cross, Christ's love)

Death 45

Winston Churchill had planned his funeral, which took place in Saint Paul's Cathedral. He included many of the great hymns of the church and used the eloquent Anglican liturgy. At his direction, a bugler, positioned high in the dome of Saint Paul's, intoned, after the benediction, the sound of "Taps," the universal signal that says the day is over.

But then came a dramatic turn: as Churchill instructed, after "Taps" was finished, another bugler, placed on the other side of the great dome, played the notes of "Reveille" —"It's time to get up. It's time to get up. It's time to get up in the morning."

That was Churchill's testimony that at the end of history, the last note will not be "Taps"; it will be "Reveille."

The worst things are never the last things.

(Resurrection, Hope)

Death 46

When John Todd, a nineteenth-century clergyman, was six years old, both his parents died. A kind-hearted aunt raised him until he left home to study for the ministry. Later, this aunt became seriously ill, and in distress she wrote Todd a letter. Would death mean the end of everything, or could she hope for something beyond? Here, condensed from *The Autobiography of John Todd*, is the letter he sent in reply:

It is now thirty-five years since I, as a boy of six, was left quite alone in the world. You sent me word you would give me a home and be a kind mother to me. I have never forgotten the day I made the long journey to your house. I can still recall my disappointment when, instead of coming for me yourself, you sent your servant, Caesar, to fetch me.

I remember my tears and anxiety as, perched high on your horse and clinging tight to Caesar, I rode off to my new home. Night fell before we finished the journey, and I became lonely and afraid. "Do you think she'll go to bed before we get there?" I asked Caesar.

"Oh no!" he said reassuringly, "She'll stay up for you. When we get out o' these here woods, you'll see her candle shinin' in the window."

Presently we did ride out into the clearing, and there, sure enough, was your candle. I remember you were waiting at the door, that you put your arms close about me—a tired and bewildered little boy. You had a fire burning on the hearth, a hot supper waiting on the stove. After supper you took me to my new room, heard me say my prayers, and then sat beside me till I fell asleep.

Some day soon God will send for you, to take you to a new home. Don't fear the summons, the strange journey, or the messenger of death. God can be trusted to do as much for you as you were kind enough to do for me so many years ago. At the end of the road you will find love and a welcome awaiting, and you will be safe in God's care.

(Hope, Heaven)

Death 47

Donald Grey Barnhouse was driving his children to the funeral of their mother. A semitractor trailer truck crossed in front of them at an intersection, momentarily casting a shadow on the car, and Barnhouse asked his children, "Would you rather be struck by the semi or the shadow?"

"The shadow, of course," they replied.

"That's what has happened to us," said Barnhouse. "Mother's dying is only the shadow of death. The lost sinner is struck by the semi of death."

(Resurrection, Lostness)

Colin Chapman, in *The Case for Christianity,* quotes Ugandan bishop Festo Kivengere's account of the 1973 execution by firing squad of three men from his diocese:

February 10 began as a sad day for us in Kabale. People were commanded to come to the stadium and witness the execution. Death permeated the atmosphere. A silent crowd of about three thousand was there to watch.

I had permission from the authorities to speak to the men before they died, and two of my fellow ministers were with me.

They brought the men in a truck and unloaded them. They were handcuffed, and their feet were chained. The firing squad stood at attention. As we walked into the center of the stadium, I was wondering what to say. How do you give the gospel to doomed men who are probably seething with rage?

We approached them from behind, and as they turned to look at us, what a sight! Their faces were all alight with an unmistakable glow and radiance. Before we could say anything, one of them burst out:

"Bishop, thank you for coming! I wanted to tell you. The day I was arrested, in my prison cell, I asked the Lord Jesus to come into my heart. He came in and forgave me all my sins! Heaven is now open, and there is nothing between me and my God! Please tell my wife and children that I am going to be with Jesus. Ask them to accept him into their lives as I did."

The other two men told similar stories, excitedly raising their hands which rattled their handcuffs.

I felt that what I needed to do was to talk to the soldiers, not to the condemned. So I translated what the men had said into a language the soldiers understood. The military men were standing there with guns cocked and bewilderment on their faces. They were so dumbfounded that they forgot to put the hoods over the men's faces!

The three faced the firing squad standing close together. They looked toward the people and began to wave, handcuffs and all. The people waved back. Then shots were fired, and the three were with Jesus.

We stood in front of them, our own hearts throbbing with joy, mingled with tears. It was a day never to be forgotten. Though dead, the men spoke loudly to all of Kigezi District and beyond, so that there was an upsurge of life in Christ, which challenges death and defeats it.

The next Sunday, I was preaching to a huge crowd in the home town of one of the executed men. Again, the feel of death was over the congregation. But when I gave them the testimony of their man, and how he died, there erupted a great song of praise to Jesus! Many turned to the Lord there.

(Joy, Witness)

Dedication 49

In the December 1987 *Life* magazine, Brad Darrach writes:

Meryl Streep is gray with cold. In *Ironweed,* her new movie, she plays a ragged derelict who dies in a cheap hotel room, and for more than half an hour before the scene she has been hugging a huge bag of ice cubes in an agonizing effort to experience how it feels to be a corpse.

Now the camera begins to turn. Jack Nicholson, her derelict lover, sobs and screams and shakes her body. But through take after take—and between takes too—Meryl just lies there like an iced mackerel. Frightened, a member of the crew whispers to the director, Hector Babenco, "What's going on? She's not breathing!"

Babenco gives a start. In Meryl's body there is absolutely no sign of life! He hesitates, then lets the scene proceed. Yet even after the shot is made and the set struck, Meryl continues to lie there, gray and still. Only after 10 minutes have passed does she slowly, slowly emerge from the coma-like state into which she has deliberately sunk.

Babenco is amazed. "Now *that,*" he mutters in amazement, "is acting! *That* is an actress!"

Total dedication amazes people. How wonderful to be so dedicated to Christ that people will say, "Now *that* is a Christian!"

(Salt, Testimony)

Denial 50

An old story tells of a desert nomad who awakened hungry in the middle of the night. He lit a candle and began eating dates from a bowl beside his bed. He took a bite from one end and saw a worm in it, so he threw it out of the tent. He bit into the second date, found another worm, and threw it away also. Reasoning that he wouldn't have any dates left to eat if he continued, he blew out the candle and quickly ate all the dates.

Many there are who prefer darkness and denial to the light of reality.

(Truth, Light)

Difficulties 51

On December 29, 1987, a Soviet cosmonaut returned to the earth after 326 days in orbit. He was in good health, which hasn't always been the case in those record-breaking voyages. Five years earlier, touching down after 211 days in space, two cosmonauts suffered from dizziness, high pulse rates, and heart palpitations. They couldn't walk for a week, and after 30 days, they were still undergoing therapy for atrophied muscles and weakened hearts.

At zero gravity, the muscles of the body begin to waste away because there is no resistance. To counteract this, the Soviets prescribed a vigorous exercise program for the cosmonauts. They invented the "penguin suit," a running suit laced with elastic bands. It resists every move the cosmonauts make, forcing them to exert their strength. Apparently the regimen is working.

We often long dreamily for days without difficulty, but God knows better. The easier our life, the weaker our spiritual fiber, for strength of any kind grows only by exertion.

(Strength, Work)

Discipleship 52

David Thomas in *Marriage and Family Living* writes:

Recently our daughter received a document of almost infinite worth to a typical fifteen-year-old: a learner's permit for driving. Shortly thereafter, I accompanied her as she drove for the first time.

In the passenger seat, having no steering wheel and no brakes, I was, in a most explicit way, in her hands—a strange feeling for a parent, both disturbing and surprisingly satisfying.

As she looked to see if the road was clear, we slowly pulled away from the curb. Meanwhile, I checked to determine not only that, but to see if the sky was falling or the earth quaking. If getting from here to there was the only thing that mattered, I would gladly have taken the wheel. But there were other matters of importance here, most of them having to do with my own paternal "letting go."

I experienced a strange combination of weakness and power. My understanding of weakness was simple: she was in control, I was not. But she was able to move to this level of adulthood because of what my wife and I had done. Our power had empowered her. Her new-found strength was attained from us. So as we pulled away from the curb, we all gained in stature.

(Parenting, Children)

Discipline 53

Dennis Miller writes:

Out of parental concern and a desire to teach our young son responsibility, we require him to phone home when he arrives at his friend's house a few blocks away. He began to forget, however, as he grew more confident in his ability to get there without disaster befalling him.

The first time he forgot, I called to be sure he had arrived. We told him the next time it happened, he would have to come home. A few days later, however, the telephone again lay silent, and I knew if he was going to learn, he would have to be punished. But I did not want to punish him! I went to the telephone, regretting that his great time would have to be spoiled by his lack of contact with his father.

As I dialed, I prayed for wisdom. "Treat him like I treat you," the Lord seemed to say. With that, as the telephone rang one time, I hung up. A few seconds later the phone rang, and it was my son. "I'm here, Dad!"

"What took you so long to call?" I asked.

"We started playing and I forgot. But Dad, I heard the phone ring once, and I remembered."

"I'm glad you remembered," I said. "Have fun."

How often do we think of God as One who waits to punish us when we step out of line? I wonder how often he rings just once, hoping we will phone home.

(Parenting, God's patience)

Distraction 54

A former police officer tells of the tactics of roving bands of thieves:

They enter the store as a group. One or two separate themselves from the group, and the others start a loud commotion in another section of the store. This grabs the attention of the clerks and customers. As all eyes are turned to the disturbance, the accomplices fill their pockets with merchandise and cash, leaving before anyone suspects.

Hours—sometimes even days—later, the victimized merchant realizes things are missing and calls the police. Too late.

How often this effective strategy is used by the Evil One! We are seduced into paying attention to the distractions, while evil agents ransack our lives.

(Satan, Priorities)

Easter 55

Margaret Sangster Phippen wrote that in the mid-1950s her father, British minister W. E. Sangster, began to notice some uneasiness in his throat and a dragging in his leg. When he went to the doctor, he found that he had an incurable disease that caused progressive muscular atrophy. His muscles would gradually waste away, his voice would fail, his throat would soon become unable to swallow.

Sangster threw himself into his work in British home missions, figuring he could still write and he would have even more time for prayer. "Let me stay in the struggle Lord," he pleaded. "I don't mind if I can no longer be a general, but give me just a regiment to lead." He wrote articles and books, and helped organize prayer cells throughout England. "I'm only in the kindergarten of suffering," he told people who pitied him.

Gradually Sangster's legs became useless. His voice went completely. But he could still hold a pen, shakily. On Easter morning, just a few weeks before he died, he wrote a letter to his daughter. In it, he said, "It is terrible to wake up on Easter morning and have no voice to shout, 'He is risen!'—but it would be still more terrible to have a voice and not want to shout."

(Praise, Suffering)

Endurance 56

Neil Orchard writes:

I was talking with a farmer about his soybean and corn crops. Rain had been abundant, and the results were evident. So his comment surprised me: "My crops are especially vulnerable. Even a short drought could have a devastating effect."

"Why?" I asked.

He explained that while we see the frequent rains as a benefit, during that time the plants are not required to push roots deeper in search of water. The roots remain near the surface. A drought would find the plants unprepared and quickly kill them.

Some Christians receive abundant "rains" of worship, fellowship, and teaching. Yet when stress enters their lives, many suddenly abandon God or think him unfaithful. Their roots have never pushed much below the surface. Only roots grown deep into God (Col. 2:6–7) help us endure times of drought in our lives.

(Prosperity, Trust)

Evangelism 57

An old man, walking the beach at dawn, noticed a young man ahead of him picking up starfish and flinging them into the sea. Catching up with the youth, he asked what he was doing. The answer was that the stranded starfish would die if left until the morning sun.

"But the beach goes on for miles, and there are millions of starfish," countered the old man. "How can your effort make a difference?"

The young man looked at the starfish in his hand and then threw it to safety in the waves. "It makes a difference to this one," he said.

(Great commission, Service)

Evangelism 58

Survivor Eva Hart remembers the night, April 15, 1912, on which the Titanic plunged 12,000 feet to the Atlantic floor, some two hours and forty minutes after an iceberg tore a 300-foot gash in the starboard side: "I saw all the horror of its sinking, and I heard, even more dreadful, the cries of drowning people."

Although twenty life-boats and rafts were launched—too few and only partly filled—most of the passengers ended up struggling in the icy seas while those in the boats waited a safe distance away.

Lifeboat No. 14 did row back to the scene after the unsinkable ship slipped from sight at 2:20 A.M. Alone, it chased cries in the darkness, seeking and saving a precious few. Incredibly, no other boat joined it. Some were already overloaded, but in virtually every other boat, those already saved rowed their half-filled boats aimlessly in the night, listening to the cries of the lost. Each feared a crush of unknown swimmers would cling to their craft, eventually swamping it.

"I came to seek and to save the lost," our Savior said. And he commissioned us to do the same. But we face a large obstacle: fear. While people drown in the treacherous waters around us, we are tempted to stay dry and make certain no one rocks the boat.

(Selfishness, Compassion)

Even if people reject the gospel, we still must love them. A good example of this was reported by Ralph Neighbour, pastor of Houston's West Memorial Baptist Church (in *Death and the Caring Community,* by Larry Richards and Paul Johnson):

Jack had been president of a large corporation, and when he got cancer, they ruthlessly dumped him. He went through his insurance, used his life savings, and had practically nothing left.

I visited him with one of my deacons, who said, "Jack, you speak so openly about the brief life you have left. I wonder if you've prepared for your life after death?"

Jack stood up, livid with rage. "You——Christians. All you ever think about is what's going to happen to me after I die. If your God is so great, why doesn't he do something about the real problems of life?" He went on to tell us he was leaving his wife penniless and his daughter without money for college. Then he ordered us out.

Later my deacon insisted we go back. We did.

"Jack, I know I offended you," he said. "I humbly apologize. But I want you to know I've been working since then. Your first problem is where your family will live after you die. A realtor in our church has agreed to sell your house and give your wife his commission.

"I guarantee you that, if you'll permit us, some other men and I will make the house payments until it's sold.

"Then, I've contacted the owner of an apartment house down the street. He's offered your wife a three-bedroom apartment plus free utilities and an $850-a-month salary in return for her collecting rents and supervising plumbing and electrical repairs. The income from your house should pay for your daughter's college. I just wanted you to know your family will be cared for."

Jack cried like a baby.

He died shortly thereafter, so wrapped in pain he never accepted Christ. But he experienced God's love even while rejecting him. And his widow, touched by the caring Christians, responded to the gospel message.

(Love, Witness)

Evangelism 60

Roger Storms, pastor of First Christian Church in Chandler, Arizona, tells this story:

One Sunday, a car had broken down in the alley behind our facilities, and the driver had jacked up the car and crawled underneath to work on the problem. Suddenly, we heard him scream for help. The jack had slipped, and the car had come down on top of him.

Someone shouted, "Call 9-1-1!" and a couple of people ran for the phone. Several of our men gathered around the large car and strained to lift it off the trapped man. Nurses from our congregation were rounded up and brought to the scene. Somehow the men were able to ease the car's weight off the man, and he was pulled free. Our nurses checked him over. He was scratched up and shaken, but otherwise okay.

When this man was in peril, people did all they could to help—risking themselves, inconveniencing themselves. Whatever was necessary to save this man, they were ready to try. How we need this same attitude when it comes to rescuing those in greatest peril—the danger of losing life eternally!

(Convenience, Sacrifice)

Evangelism 61

One Mercedes Benz TV commercial shows their car colliding with a cement wall during a safety test. Someone then asks the company spokesman why they do not enforce their patent on the Mercedes Benz energy-absorbing car body, a design evidently copied by other companies because of its success.

He replies matter-of-factly, "Because some things in life are too important not to share."

How true. In that category also falls the gospel of salvation, which saves people from far more than auto collisions.

(Gospel, Selfishness)

Evangelism 62

On July 15, 1986, Roger Clemens, the sizzling right-hander for the Boston Red Sox, started his first All-Star Game. In the second inning he came to bat, something he hadn't done in years because of the American League's designated-hitter rule. He took a few uncertain practice swings and then looked out at his forbidding opponent, Dwight Gooden, who the previous year had won the Cy Young award.

Gooden wound up and threw a white-hot fastball past Clemens. With an embarrassed smile on his face, Clemens stepped out of the box and asked catcher Gary Carter, "Is that what my pitches look like?"

"You bet it is!" replied Carter. Although Clemens quickly struck out, he went on to pitch three perfect innings and be named the game's most valuable player. From that day on, he later said, with a fresh reminder of how overpowering a good fastball is, he pitched with far greater boldness.

Sometimes we forget the Holy Spirit within us and how powerful our witness can be. The gospel has supernatural power—when we speak it in confidence.

(Gospel, Boldness)

Excellence 63

Gene Stallings tells of an incident when he was defensive backfield coach of the Dallas Cowboys. Two All-Pro players, Charlie Waters and Cliff Harris, were sitting in front of their lockers after playing a tough game against the Washington Redskins. They were still in their uniforms, and their heads were bowed in exhaustion. Waters said to Harris, "By the way Cliff, what was the final score?"

As these men show, excellence isn't determined by comparing our score to someone else's. Excellence comes from giving one's best, no matter the score.

(Winning, Competition)

Excellence 64

Integrity is more than not being deceitful or slipshod. It means doing everything "heartily as unto the Lord" (Col. 3:23). In his book *Lyrics,* Oscar Hammerstein II points out one reason why, a reason Christians have always known:

A year or so ago, on the cover of the New York *Herald Tribune* Sunday magazine, I saw a picture of the Statue of Liberty . . . taken from a helicopter, and it showed the top of the statue's head. I was amazed to see the detail there. The sculptor had done a painstaking job with the lady's coiffure, and yet he must have been pretty sure that the only eyes that would see this detail would be the uncritical eyes of sea gulls. He could not have dreamt that any man would ever fly over this head. He was artist enough, however, to finish off this part of the statue with as much care as he had devoted to her face and her arms and the torch and everything that people can see as they sail up the bay. . . .

When you are creating a work of art, or any other kind of work, finish the job off perfectly. You never know when a helicopter, or some other instrument not at the moment invented, may come along and find you out.

(Service, Finishing)

Failure 65

Fred Astaire was without dispute one of the top singers, dancers, and actors of all time. In *Top Hat, Swing Time, Holiday Inn,* and other famous movies, he danced and crooned his way into people's hearts worldwide.

But in 1932, when Astaire was starting out, a Hollywood talent judge wrote on his screen test: "Can't act. Can't sing. Can dance a little."

As Christians, we may fail badly. *What kind of a Christian would do that?* we think. *How can I ever serve Christ again?*

But we develop in the Christian life when we leave those failures behind and daily use our God-given gifts for him. In time, those failures will be forgotten footnotes.

(Spiritual gifts, Perseverance)

Faith 66

An illustration of the balance between faith and works lies hidden within any tree. Leaves use up nutrients in the process of photosynthesis. As the leaves consume nutrients in the sap, a suction is formed, which draws more sap from the roots. Without the sap, the leaves and branches would die. But the continual flow of this sap comes only as it is used up by the work of the leaf.

Likewise, through faith we draw life from Christ. But a continual supply of fresh spiritual nutrients depends on our willingness to "consume" the old supply through our acts of obedience, through our works.

(Good works, Power)

Faith 67

In April 1988 the evening news reported on a photographer who was a skydiver. He had jumped from a plane along with numerous other skydivers and filmed the group as they fell and opened their parachutes. On the film shown on the telecast, as the final skydiver opened his chute, the picture went berserk. The announcer reported that the cameraman had fallen to his death, having jumped out of the plane without his parachute. It wasn't until he reached for the absent ripcord that he realized he was freefalling without a parachute.

Until that point, the jump probably seemed exciting and fun. But tragically, he had acted with thoughtless haste and deadly foolishness. Nothing could save him, for his faith was in a parachute never buckled on. Faith in anything but an all-sufficient God can be just as tragic spiritually. Only with faith in Jesus Christ dare we step into the dangerous excitement of life.

(Self-reliance, Preparation)

Faith 68

The African impala can jump to a height of over 10 feet and cover a distance of greater than 30 feet. Yet these magnificent creatures can be kept in an enclosure in any zoo with a 3-foot wall. The animals will not jump if they cannot see where their feet will fall.

Faith is the ability to trust what we cannot see, and with faith we are freed from the flimsy enclosures of life that only fear allows to entrap us.

(Spiritual perception, Vision)

Faith 69

This piece was heard on National Public Radio's *Morning Edition* on November 2, 1988:

In 1958, America's first commercial jet air service began with the flight of the Boeing 707. A month after that first flight, a traveler on a piston-engine, propeller-driven DC-6 airliner struck up a conversation with a fellow passenger. The passenger happened to be a Boeing engineer. The traveler asked the engineer about the new jet aircraft, whereupon the engineer began speaking at length about the extensive testing Boeing had done on the jet engine before bringing it into commercial service. He recounted Boeing's experience with engines, from the B-17 to the B-52.

When his traveling companion asked him if he himself had yet flown on the new 707 jet airliner, the engineer replied, "I think I'll wait until it's been in service awhile."

Even enthusiastic talking about our faith doesn't mean much if we aren't also willing to put our lives where our mouth is.

(Trust, Testimony)

Faith 70

Donner Atwood, in *Reformed Review,* writes:

During the terrible days of the Blitz, a father, holding his small son by the hand, ran from a building that had been struck by a bomb. In the front yard was a shell hole. Seeking shelter as soon as possible, the father jumped into the hole and held up his arms for his son to follow.

Terrified, yet hearing his father's voice telling him to jump, the boy replied, "I can't see you!"

The father, looking up against the sky tinted red by the burning buildings, called to the silhouette of his son, "But I can see you. Jump!"

The boy jumped, because he trusted his father.

The Christian faith enables us to face life or meet death, not because we can see, but with the certainty that we are seen; not that we know all the answers, but that we are known.

(Father God, God's knowledge)

Faith 71

Imagine a family of mice who lived all their lives in a large piano. To them in their piano-world came the music of the instrument, filling all the dark spaces with sound and harmony. At first the mice were impressed by it. They drew comfort and wonder from the thought that there was Someone who made the music—though invisible to them—above, yet close to them. They loved to think of the Great Player whom they could not see.

Then one day a daring mouse climbed up part of the piano and returned very thoughtful. He had found out how music was made. Wires were the secret; tightly stretched wires of graduated lengths which trembled and vibrated. They must revise all their old beliefs: none but the most conservative could any longer believe in the Unseen Player.

Later, another explorer carried the explanation further. Hammers were now the secret, numbers of hammers dancing and leaping on the wires. This was a more complicated theory, but it all went to show that they lived in a purely mechanical and mathematical world. The Unseen Player came to be thought of as a myth.

But the pianist continued to play.

—Reprinted from *The London Observer*

(Doubt, God's sovereignty)

Fall, of man 72

Brent Philip Waters in *The Christian Ministry* writes:

A favorite nursery rhyme is the familiar tale of an egg that takes an unfortunate tumble:

Humpty Dumpty sat on a wall, Humpty Dumpty had a great fall. All the king's horses and all the king's men couldn't put Humpty together again.

According to those who know about such things, this piece of wisdom is a relic thousands of years old. Versions have appeared in eight European languages.

In its primitive stages, however, Humpty Dumpty was a riddle. It asked the question: what, when broken, can never be repaired, not even by strong or wise individuals? As any child knows, an egg. Regardless of how hard we try, a broken egg can never be put back together again. We simply have to learn to live with the mess.

There is a Humpty Dumpty story in the Bible. We call it the Fall.

Adam and Eve eat the forbidden fruit. They claim they possess the necessary wisdom to be like God. When the dust settles, Adam and Eve are not perched on a lofty plane. They have fallen. Regardless of how hard we try, things can never be put back together again.

Our contemporary fall is seen in the feeling that things just don't work anymore. Our lives appear out of control. Changes come faster than our ability to cope. Broken eggs are an appropriate symbol. Wherever we step we hear the crunch of fragile shells beneath our feet.

(Brokenness, Sin)

Fathers 73

In *The Effective Father,* Gordon MacDonald writes:

It is said of Boswell, the famous biographer of Samuel Johnson, that he often referred to a special day in his childhood when his father took him fishing. The day was fixed in his mind, and he often reflected upon many things his father had taught him in the course of their fishing experience together.

After having heard of that particular excursion so often, it occurred to someone much later to check the journal that Boswell's father kept and determine what had been said about the fishing trip from the parental perspective. Turning to that date, the reader found only one sentence entered: "Gone fishing today with my son; a day wasted."

(Children, Teaching)

Father's Day 74

A grown man awaiting surgery in the hospital was talking with his father. "Dad," he said, "I sure hope I can be home for Father's Day. I felt awful years ago when I was 10, because I never gave you a gift that year."

The father replied, "Mark, I remember that Saturday before Father's Day. I saw you in the store. I watched as you picked up the cigars and stuffed them in your pocket. I knew you had no money, and I was sad because I thought you were going to run out of the store without paying. But as soon as you hid the cigars, you pulled them out and put them back.

"When you stayed out playing all the next day because you had no present, you probably thought I was hurt. You're wrong. When you put the cigars back and decided not to break the law, Mark, you gave me the best present I ever received."

(Honesty, Gifts)

Favoritism 75

A Chicago bank once asked for a letter of recommendation on a young Bostonian being considered for employment.

The Boston investment house could not say enough about the young man. His father, they wrote, was a Cabot; his mother was a Lowell. Further back was a happy blend of Saltonstalls, Peabodys, and others of Boston's finest families. His recommendation was given without hesitation.

Several days later, the Chicago bank sent a note saying the information supplied was altogether inadequate. It read: "We are not contemplating using the young man for breeding purposes. Just for work."

Neither is God a respecter of persons but uses those from every family, nation, and race who want to work for his kingdom.

(Partiality, Service)

Fear 76

Picture this: Eric Valli, a professional photographer, is dangling by a nylon rope from a 395-foot cliff in Nepal. Nearby on a rope ladder is another man, Mani Lal, doing what he has done for decades: hunting honey. Here in the Himalayan foothills, the cliffs shelter honeycombs of the world's largest honeybee.

At the moment, thousands of them are buzzing around both men. Lal, a veteran of hundreds of such attacks, is calm. Not so Mr. Valli. Describing that moment in *National Geographic,* he says, "There were so many bees I was afraid I might freak out. But I knew if I did, I would be dead. So I took a deep breath and relaxed. Getting stung would be better than finding myself at the bottom of the cliff." He overcame his fears and won a photo competition for his efforts.

Fear can send a person plummeting to destruction. Some believers, fearing the stings of persecution, testing, and temptation, have compromised their faith and slipped from the lifeline of Christ—which is why the Bible teaches us to fear God alone.

(Reverence, Persecution)

Fellowship 77

In the fall of the year, Linda, a young woman, was traveling alone up the rutted and rugged highway from Alberta to the Yukon. Linda didn't know you don't travel to Whitehorse alone in a rundown Honda Civic, so she set off where only four-wheel-drives normally venture. The first evening she found a room in the mountains near a summit and asked for a 5 A.M. wakeup call so she could get an early start. She couldn't understand why the clerk looked surprised at that request, but as she awoke to early-morning fog shrouding the mountain tops, she understood.

Not wanting to look foolish, she got up and went to breakfast. Two truckers invited Linda to join them, and since the place was so small, she felt obliged. "Where are you headed?" one of the truckers asked.

"Whitehorse."

"In that little Civic? No way! This pass is *dangerous* in weather like this."

"Well, I'm determined to try," was Linda's gutsy, if not very informed, response.

"Then I guess we're just going to have to hug you," the trucker suggested.

Linda drew back. "There's no way I'm going to let you touch me!"

"Not like that!" The truckers chuckled. "We'll put one truck in front of you and one in the rear. In that way, we'll get you through the mountains." All that foggy morning Linda followed the two red dots in front of her and had the reassurance of a big escort behind as they made their way safely through the mountains.

Caught in the fog in our dangerous passage through life, we need to be "hugged." With fellow Christians who know the way and can lead safely ahead of us, and with others behind, gently encouraging us along, we, too, can pass safely.

(Church, Accountability)

Fighting 78

National Geographic included a photograph of the fossil remains of two saber-toothed cats locked in combat. To quote the article: "One had bitten deep into the leg bone of the other, a thrust that trapped both in a common fate. The cause of the death of the two cats is as clear as the causes of extinction of their species are obvious."

When Christians fight each other, everybody loses. As Paul put it, "If you keep on biting and devouring each other, watch out or you will be destroyed by each other" (Gal. 5:15).

(Conflict, Forgiveness)

Forgiveness 79

Richard Hoefler's book *Will Daylight Come?* includes a homey illustration of how sin enslaves and forgiveness frees.

A little boy visiting his grandparents was given his first slingshot. He practiced in the woods, but he could never hit his target.

As he came back to Grandma's back yard, he spied her pet duck. On an impulse he took aim and let fly. The stone hit, and the duck fell dead.

The boy panicked. Desperately he hid the dead duck in the woodpile, only to look up and see his sister watching. Sally had seen it all, but she said nothing.

After lunch that day, Grandma said, "Sally, let's wash the dishes."

But Sally said, "Johnny told me he wanted to help in the kitchen today. Didn't you, Johnny?" And she whispered to him, "Remember the duck!" So Johnny did the dishes.

Later Grandpa asked if the children wanted to go fishing. Grandma said, "I'm sorry, but I need Sally to help make supper." Sally smiled and said, "That's all taken care of. Johnny wants to do it." Again she whispered, "Remember the duck." Johnny stayed while Sally went fishing.

After several days of Johnny doing both his chores and Sally's, finally he couldn't stand it. He confessed to Grandma that he'd killed the duck.

"I know, Johnny," she said, giving him a hug. "I was standing at the window and saw the whole thing. Because I love you, I forgave you. I wondered how long you would let Sally make a slave of you."

(Confession, Bondage)

Forgiveness 80

In an article in *Guideposts,* Corrie ten Boom told of not being able to forget a wrong that had been done to her. She had forgiven the person, but she kept rehashing the incident and so, couldn't sleep. Finally Corrie cried out to God for help in putting the problem to rest. She writes:

His help came in the form of a kindly Lutheran pastor to whom I confessed my failure after two sleepless weeks. "Up in that church tower," he said, nodding out the window, "is a bell which is rung by pulling on a rope. But you know what? After the sexton lets go of the rope the bell keeps on swinging. First 'ding,' then 'dong.' Slower and slower until there's a final dong and it stops. I believe the same thing is true of forgiveness. When we forgive, we take our hand off the rope. But if we've been tugging at our grievances for a long time, we mustn't be surprised if the old angry thoughts keep coming for a while. They're just the ding-dongs of the old bell slowing down."

And so it proved to be. There were a few more midnight reverberations, a couple of dings when the subject came up in my conversations. But the force—which was my willingness in the matter—had gone out of them. They came less and less often and at last stopped altogether. And so I discovered another secret of forgiveness: we can trust God not only above our emotions, but also above our thoughts.

(Emotions, Memories)

Forgiveness 81

In his book, *Lee: The Last Years,* Charles Bracelen Flood reports that after the Civil War, Robert E. Lee visited a Kentucky lady who took him to the remains of a grand old tree in front of her house. There she bitterly cried that its limbs and trunk had been destroyed by Federal Artillery fire. She looked to Lee for a word condemning the North or at least sympathizing with her loss.

After a brief silence, Lee said, "Cut it down, my dear Madam, and forget it."

It is better to forgive the injustices of the past than to allow them to remain, let bitterness take root, and poison the rest of our life.

(Bitterness, Injustice)

Forgiveness 82

Senator Mark Hatfield recounts the following history:

James Garfield was a lay preacher and principal of his denominational college. They say he was ambidextrous and could simultaneously write Greek with one hand and Latin with the other.

In 1880, he was elected president of the United States, but after only six months in office, he was shot in the back with a revolver. He never lost consciousness. At the hospital, the doctor probed the wound with his little finger to seek the bullet. He couldn't find it, so he tried a silver-tipped probe. Still he couldn't locate the bullet.

They took Garfield back to Washington, D.C. Despite the summer heat, they tried to keep him comfortable. He was growing very weak. Teams of doctors tried to locate the bullet, probing the wound over and over. In desperation they asked Alexander Graham Bell, who was working on a little device called the telephone to see if he could locate the metal inside the president's body. He came, he sought, and he too failed.

The president hung on through July, through August, but in September he finally died—not from the wound but from infection. The repeated probing, which the physicians thought would help the man, eventually killed him.

So it is with people who dwell too long on their sin and refuse to release it to God.

(Sin, Christ's work)

Freedom 83

Charles Simpson, in *Pastoral Renewal,* writes:

I met a young man not long ago who dives for exotic fish for aquariums. He said one of the most popular aquarium fish is the shark. He explained that if you catch a small shark and confine it, it will stay a size proportionate to the aquarium. Sharks can be six inches long yet fully matured. But if you turn them loose in the ocean, they grow to their normal length of eight feet.

That also happens to some Christians. I've seen the cutest little six-inch Christians who swim around in a little puddle. But if you put them into a larger arena—into the whole creation—only then can they become great.

(Missions, Growth)

Giving 84

Charles Spurgeon and his wife, according to a story in *The Chaplain* magazine, would sell, but refused to give away, the eggs their chickens laid. Even close relatives were told, "You may have them if you pay for them." As a result, some people labeled the Spurgeons greedy and grasping.

They accepted the criticisms without defending themselves, and only after Mrs. Spurgeon died was the full story revealed: All the profits from the sale of eggs went to support two elderly widows. Because the Spurgeons were unwilling to let their left hand know what the right hand was doing (Matt. 6:3), they endured the attacks in silence.

(Money, Good works)

Giving 85

In Other Words, a publication of the Wycliffe Bible Translators, recently told a story about Sadie Sieker, who served for many years as a house-parent for missionaries' children in the Philippines.

Sadie loved books. Though she gladly loaned out some, others she treasured in a footlocker under her bed. Once, in the quiet of the night, Sadie heard a faint gnawing sound. After searching all around her room, she discovered that the noise was coming from her footlocker. When she opened it, she found nothing but an enormous pile of dust. All the books she had kept to herself had been lost to termites.

What we give away, we keep. What we hoard, we lose.

(Selfishness, Treasures)

Goals 86

It was a fog-shrouded morning, July 4, 1952, when a young woman named Florence Chadwick waded into the water off Catalina Island. She intended to swim the channel from the island to the California coast. Long-distance swimming was not new to her; she had been the first woman to swim the English Channel in both directions.

The water was numbing cold that day. The fog was so thick she could hardly see the boats in her party. Several times sharks had to be driven away with rifle fire. She swam more than fifteen hours before she asked to be taken out of the water. Her trainer tried to encourage her to swim on since they were so close to land, but when Florence looked, all she saw was fog. So she quit . . . only one-half mile from her goal.

Later she said, "I'm not excusing myself, but if I could have seen the land, I might have made it." It wasn't the cold or fear or exhaustion that caused Florence Chadwick to fail. It was the fog.

Many times we too fail, not because we're afraid or because of the peer pressure or because of anything other than the fact that we lose sight of the goal. Maybe that's why Paul said, "I press toward the mark for the prize of the high calling of God in Christ Jesus" (Phil. 3:14).

Two months after her failure, Florence Chadwick walked off the same beach into the same channel and swam the distance, setting a new speed record, because she could see the land.

(Failure, Perseverance)

God's goodness 87

Everyone is familiar with Sherlock Holmes, his faithful companion Dr. Watson, and Holmes's keen power of observation that solved countless crimes. Yet few of us know that Holmes thought deduction and observation were even more necessary to religion.

Tucked away in *The Adventure of the Naval Treaty,* Holmes is found studying a rose. Watson narrates: "He walked past the couch to an open window and held up the drooping stalk of a moss rose, looking down at the dainty blend of crimson and green. It was a new phase of his character to me, for I had never before seen him show an interest in natural objects."

" 'There is nothing in which deduction is so necessary as in religion,' said he, leaning with his back against the shutters. . . . 'Our highest assurance of the goodness of Providence seems to me to rest in the flowers. All other things, our powers, our desires, our food, are really necessary for our existence in the first instance. But this rose is an extra. Its smell and its color are an embellishment of life, not a condition of it. It is only goodness which gives extras, and so I say again that we have much to hope from the flowers.' "

What other "extras" should we be observing and thanking God for this year?

(Thankfulness, Faith)

God's pursuit 88

Several years ago an eastern paper reported this story:

One evening a woman was driving home when she noticed a huge truck behind her that was driving uncomfortably close. She stepped on the gas to gain some distance from the truck, but when she sped up, the truck did too. The faster she drove, the faster the truck did.

Now scared, she exited the freeway. But the truck stayed with her. The woman then turned up a main street, hoping to lose her pursuer in traffic. But the truck ran a red light and continued the chase.

Reaching the point of panic, the woman whipped her car into a service station and bolted out of her auto screaming for help. The truck driver sprang from his truck and ran toward her car. Yanking the back door open, the driver pulled out a man hidden in the back seat.

The woman was running from the wrong person. From his high vantage point, the truck driver had spotted a would-be rapist in the woman's car. The chase was not his effort to harm her but to save her even at the cost of his own safety.

Likewise, many people run from God, fearing what he might do to them. But his plans are for good not evil—to rescue us from the hidden sins that endanger our lives.

(God's goodness, Sin)

God's work 89

Gregory Wiens writes:

One afternoon while playing on a wooden picnic table, 4 1/2-year-old Jordon ran a splinter into his finger. Sobbing, he called his father (me) at the office. "I want God to take the splinter out," he said.

I told him his mother could remove it very easily. But he wanted God to do it because when Mom takes a splinter out, it hurts. He wanted God to remove it "by himself."

When I got home an hour later, the splinter was still there so I proceeded to remove it, and I tried to teach Jordon that sometimes God uses others to do his work. And sometimes it is painful.

(Church, Healing)

Grace 90

In Warren Wiersbe's *Meet Yourself in the Psalms,* he tells about a frontier town where a horse bolted and ran away with a wagon carrying a little boy. Seeing the child in danger, a young man risked his life to catch the horse and stop the wagon.

The child who was saved grew up to become a lawless man, and one day he stood before a judge to be sentenced for a serious crime. The prisoner recognized the judge as the man who, years before, had saved his life; so he pled for mercy on the basis of that experience.

But the words from the bench silenced his plea, "Young man, then I was your savior; today I am your judge, and I must sentence you to be hanged."

One day Jesus will say to rebellious sinners, "During that long day of grace, I was the Savior, and I would have forgiven you. But today I am your Judge. Depart from me, ye cursed, into everlasting fire!"

(Judgment, Salvation)

Grace 91

Lillie Baltrip is a good bus driver. In fact, according to the Fort Worth *Star-Telegram* of June 17, 1988, the Houston school district nominated her for a safe-driving award. Her colleagues even trusted her to drive a busload of them to an awards ceremony for safe drivers. Unfortunately, on the way to the ceremony, Lillie turned a corner too sharply and flipped the bus over, sending herself and sixteen others to the hospital for minor emergency treatment.

Did Lillie, accident free for the whole year, get her award anyway? No. Award committees rarely operate on the principle of grace. How fortunate we are that even when we don't maintain a spotless life-record, our final reward depends on God's grace, not on our performance!

(Good works, Failure)

Grace 92

Belden C. Lane writes in the *Christian Century* about English raconteur T. H. White, who recalls in *The Book of Merlyn* a boyhood experience:

"My father made me a wooden castle big enough to get into, and he fixed real pistol barrels beneath its battlements to fire a salute on my birthday, but made me sit in front the first night . . . to receive the salute, and I, believing I was to be shot, cried."

How many times have we, too, misinterpreted the ambiguity of life and thought ourselves to be "shot" when delight was intended?

One translation of Psalm 94:19 reads, "In the middle of all my troubles, you roll me over with rollicking delight." The psalmist is right; God's festive gaiety is somehow to be discerned in the midst of our own troubled fears. God often plays rough before breaking into laughter, and only a bold and rowdy playfulness can draw the whole of what we are to such a God. Yet, we're not always able to grasp the truth. Ever expecting to be shot, we are so often dumbfounded by a grace we can't conceive.

(Fear, Trials)

Greed 93

A chapter heading in Calvin Miller's book *A Requiem for Love* reads:

A beggar asked a millionaire,
"How many more dollars
Would it take to
Make you truly happy?"

The millionaire,
Reaching his gnarled hands
Into the beggar's cup, replied,
"Only one more!"

(Money, Happiness)

Greed 94

Clovis Chappell writes in his book of sermons *Feminine Faces:*

When Pompeii was being excavated, there was found a body that had been embalmed by the ashes of Vesuvius. It was that of a woman. Her feet were turned toward the city gate, but her face was turned backward toward something that lay just beyond her outstretched hands.

The prize for which those frozen fingers were reaching was a bag of pearls. Maybe she herself had dropped them as she was fleeing for her life. Maybe she had found them where they had been dropped by another. But, be that as it may, though death was hard at her heels, and life was beckoning to her beyond the city gates, she could not shake off their spell. She had turned to pick them up, with death as her reward. But it was not the eruption of Vesuvius that made her love pearls more than life. It only froze her in this attitude of greed.

(Treasures, Possessions)

Grief 95

Author Edgar Jackson poignantly describes grief:

Grief is a young widow trying to raise her three children, alone.

Grief is the man so filled with shocked uncertainty and confusion that he strikes out at the nearest person.

Grief is a mother walking daily to a nearby cemetery to stand quietly and alone a few minutes before going about the tasks of the day. She knows that a part of her is in the cemetery, just as part of her is in her daily work.

Grief is the silent, knife-like terror and sadness that comes a hundred times a day, when you start to speak to someone who is no longer there.

Grief is the emptiness that comes when you eat alone after eating with another for many years.

Grief is teaching yourself to go to bed without saying good night to the one who has died.

Grief is the helpless wishing that things were different when you know they are not and never will be again.

Grief is a whole cluster of adjustments, apprehensions, and uncertainties that strike life in its forward progress and make it difficult to redirect the energies of life.

(Death, Mourning)

Guidance 96

In *A Slow and Certain Light,* Elisabeth Elliot tells of two adventurers who stopped by to see her, all loaded with equipment for the rain forest east of the Andes. They sought no advice, just a few phrases to converse with the Indians.

She writes: "Sometimes we come to God as the two adventurers came to me—confident and, we think, well-informed and well-equipped. But has it occurred to us that with all our accumulation of stuff, something is missing?"

She suggests that we often ask God for too little. "We know what we need—a yes or no answer, please, to a simple question. Or perhaps a road sign. Something quick and easy to point the way.

"What we really ought to have is the Guide himself. Maps, road signs, a few useful phrases are good things, but infinitely better is Someone who has been there before and knows the way."

(Prayer, Direction)

Guidance 97

Perhaps you have spent some time in a sailboat. Relying on the boat to stay afloat, you slide across the water propelled by a gentle breeze. Yet within the confines of the shores, you have the opportunity and responsibility of guiding the rudder to determine the direction of travel.

Is that not similar to living within the will of God? As Christians we must rest upon God to sustain us, and upon the breath of his Spirit to empower us. Yet within his moral boundaries, we each have the opportunity and responsibility to determine our course.

(God's will, Decisions)

Bob Mumford, in *Take Another Look at Guidance,* compares discovering God's will with a sea captain's docking procedure:

A certain harbor in Italy can be reached only by sailing up a narrow channel between dangerous rocks and shoals. Over the years, many ships have been wrecked, and navigation is hazardous.

To guide the ships safely into port, three lights have been mounted on three huge poles in the harbor. When the three lights are perfectly lined up and seen as one, the ship can safely proceed up the narrow channel. If the pilot sees two or three lights, he knows he's off course and in danger.

God has also provided three beacons to guide us. The same rules of navigation apply—the three lights must be lined up before it is safe for us to proceed. The three harbor lights of guidance are:

1. The Word of God (objective standard)
2. The Holy Spirit (subjective witness)
3. Circumstances (divine providence)

Together they assure us that the directions we've received are from God and will lead us safely along his way.

(God's will, Holy Spirit)

In *Fearfully and Wonderfully Made,* Dr. Paul Brand and Philip Yancey write:

Amputees often experience some sensation of a phantom limb. Somewhere, locked in their brains, a memory lingers of the nonexistent hand or leg. Invisible toes curl, imaginary hands grasp things, a "leg" feels so sturdy a patient may try to stand on it.

For a few, the experience includes pain. Doctors watch helplessly, for the part of the body screaming for attention does not exist.

One such patient was my medical school administrator, Mr. Barwick, who had a serious and painful circulation problem in his leg but refused to allow the recommended amputation.

As the pain grew worse, Barwick grew bitter.

"I hate it! I hate it!" he would mutter about the leg. At last he relented and told the doctor, "I can't stand it anymore. I'm through with that leg. Take it off." Surgery was scheduled immediately.

Before the operation, however, Barwick asked the doctor, "What do you do with legs after they're removed?"

"We may take a biopsy or explore them a bit, but afterwards we incinerate them," the doctor replied.

Barwick proceeded with a bizarre request: "I would like you to preserve my leg in a pickling jar. I will install it on my mantle shelf. Then, as I sit in my armchair, I will taunt that leg, 'Hah! You can't hurt me anymore!' "

Ultimately, he got his wish. But the despised leg had the last laugh.

Barwick suffered phantom limb pain of the worst degree. The wound healed, but he could feel the torturous pressure of the swelling as the muscles cramped, and he had no prospect of relief. He had hated the leg with such intensity that the pain had unaccountably lodged permanently in his brain.

To me, phantom limb pain provides wonderful insight into the phenomenon of false guilt. Christians can be obsessed by the memory of some sin committed years ago. It never leaves them, crippling their ministry, their devotional life, their relationships with others. They live in fear that someone will discover their past. They work overtime trying to prove to God they're truly repentant. They erect barriers against the enveloping, loving grace of God.

Unless they experience the truth in 1 John 3:19–20 that "God is greater than our conscience," they become as pitiful as poor Mr. Barwick, shaking a fist in fury at the pickled leg on the mantle.

(Conscience, Forgiveness)

Habits 100

In *Pulpit Digest* William H. Willimon used this illustration:

Philip Haille wrote of the little village of Le Chambon in France, a town whose people, unlike others in France, hid their Jews from the Nazis. Haille went there, wondering what sort of courageous, ethical heroes could risk all to do such extraordinary good. He interviewed people in the village and was overwhelmed by their *ordinariness.* They weren't heroes or smart, discerning people.

Haille decided that the one factor that united them was their attendance, Sunday after Sunday, at their little church, where they heard the sermons of Pastor Trochme. Over time, they became by habit people who just knew what to do and did it. When it came time for them to be courageous, the day the Nazis came to town, they quietly did what was right.

One old woman, who faked a heart attack when the Nazis came to search her house, later said, "Pastor always taught us that there comes a time in every life when a person is asked to do something for Jesus. When our time came, we knew what to do."

The habits of the heart are there when they are most needed.

(Courage, Church attendance)

Heaven 101

John M. Drescher, in *Pulpit Digest,* writes:

When John Owen, the great Puritan, lay on his deathbed his secretary wrote (in his name) to a friend, "I am still in the land of the living."

"Stop," said Owen. "Change that and say, 'I am yet in the land of the dying, but I hope soon to be in the land of the living.' "

(Death, Eternal life)

Hindrances 102

In Jules Verne's novel *The Mysterious Island,* he tells of five men who escape a Civil War prison camp by hijacking a hot-air balloon. As they rise into the air, they realize the wind is carrying them over the ocean. Watching their homeland disappear on the horizon, they wonder how much longer the balloon can stay aloft.

As the hours pass and the surface of the ocean draws closer, the men decide they must cast overboard some of the weight, for they had no way to heat the air in the balloon. Shoes, overcoats, and weapons are reluctantly discarded, and the uncomfortable aviators feel their balloon rise. But only temporarily. Soon they find themselves dangerously close to the waves again, so they toss their food. Better to be high and hungry than drown on a full belly!

Unfortunately, this, too, is only a temporary solution, and the craft again threatens to lower the men into the sea. One man has an idea: they can tie the ropes that hold the passenger car and sit on those ropes. Then they can cut away the basket beneath them. As they sever the very thing they had been standing on, it drops into the ocean, and the balloon rises.

Not a minute too soon, they spot land. Eager to stand on terra firma again, the five jump into the water and swim to the island. They live, spared because they were able to discern the difference between what really was needed and what was not. The "necessities" they once thought they couldn't live without were the very weights that almost cost them their lives.

The writer to the Hebrews says, "Let us throw off everything that hinders and the sin that so easily entangles" (Heb. 12:1).

(Priorities, Sin)

Holding on 103

On a commuter flight from Portland, Maine, to Boston, Henry Dempsey, the pilot, heard an unusual noise near the rear of the small aircraft. He turned the controls over to his co-pilot and went back to check it out.

As he reached the tail section, the plane hit an air pocket, and Dempsey was tossed against the rear door. He quickly discovered the source of the mysterious noise. The rear door had not been properly latched prior to takeoff, and it flew open. He was instantly sucked out of the jet.

The co-pilot, seeing the red light that indicated an open door, radioed the nearest airport, requesting permission to make an emergency landing. He reported that the pilot had fallen out of the plane, and he requested a helicopter search of that area of the ocean.

After the plane landed, they found Henry Dempsey—holding onto the outdoor ladder of the aircraft. Somehow he had caught the ladder, held on for ten minutes as the plane flew 200 mph at an altitude of 4,000 feet, and then, at landing, kept his head from hitting the runway, which was a mere twelve inches away. It took airport personnel several minutes to pry Dempsey's fingers from the ladder.

Things in life may be turbulent, and you may not feel like holding on. But have you considered the alternative?

(Perseverance, Trials)

Gordon Brownville's *Symbols of the Holy Spirit* tells about the great Norwegian explorer Roald Amundsen, the first to discover the magnetic meridian of the North Pole and to discover the South Pole. On one of his trips, Amundsen took a homing pigeon with him. When he had finally reached the top of the world, he opened the bird's cage and set it free.

Imagine the delight of Amundsen's wife, back in Norway, when she looked up from the doorway of her home and saw the pigeon circling in the sky above. No doubt she exclaimed, "He's alive! My husband is still alive!"

So it was when Jesus ascended. He was gone, but the disciples clung to his promise to send them the Holy Spirit. What joy, then, when the dovelike Holy Spirit descended at Pentecost. The disciples had with them the continual reminder that Jesus was alive and victorious at the right hand of the Father. This continues to be the Spirit's message.

(Christ's ascension, Signs)

Honesty 105

In his book *Integrity,* Ted Engstrom tells this story:

For Coach Cleveland Stroud and the Bulldogs of Rockdale County High School [Conyers, Georgia], it was their championship season: 21 wins and 5 losses on the way to the Georgia boy's basketball tournament last March, then a dramatic come-from-behind victory in the state finals.

But now the new glass trophy case outside the high school gymnasium is bare. Earlier this month the Georgia High School Association deprived Rockdale County of the championship after school officials said that a player who was scholastically ineligible had played 45 seconds in the first of the school's five postseason games.

"We didn't know he was ineligible at the time; we didn't know it until a few weeks ago," Mr. Stroud said. "Some people have said we should have just kept quiet about it, that it was just 45 seconds and the player wasn't an impact player. But you've got to do what's honest and right and what the rules say. I told my team that people forget the scores of basketball games; they don't ever forget what you're made of."

(Integrity, Reputation)

Humility 106

The *Handbook of Magazine Article Writing* contains this illustration by Philip Barry Osborne:

Alex Haley, the author of *Roots,* has a picture in his office, showing a turtle sitting atop a fence. The picture is there to remind him of a lesson he learned long ago: "If you see a turtle on a fence post, you know he had some help."

Says Alex, "Any time I start thinking, *Wow, isn't this marvelous what I've done!* I look at that picture and remember how this turtle—me—got up on that post."

(Help, Success)

Hypocrisy 107

The *Queen Mary* was the largest ship to cross the oceans when it was launched in 1936. Through four decades and a world war she served until she was retired, anchored as a floating hotel and museum in Long Beach, California.

During the conversion, her three massive smokestacks were taken off to be scraped down and repainted. But on the dock they crumbled.

Nothing was left of the 3/4-inch steel plate from which the stacks had been formed. All that remained were more than thirty coats of paint that had been applied over the years. The steel had rusted away.

When Jesus called the Pharisees "whitewashed tombs," he meant they had no substance, only an exterior appearance.

(Appearances, Character)

Independence 108

On November 20, 1988, the *Los Angeles Times* reported:

A screaming woman, trapped in a car dangling from a freeway transition road in East Los Angeles was rescued Saturday morning. The 19-year-old woman apparently fell asleep behind the wheel about 12:15 A.M. The car, which plunged through a guard rail was left dangling by its left rear wheel. A half dozen passing motorists stopped, grabbed some ropes from one of their vehicles, tied the ropes to the back of the woman's car, and hung on until the fire units arrived. A ladder was extended from below to help stabilize the car while firefighters tied the vehicle to tow trucks with cables and chains.

"Every time we would move the car," said one of the rescuers, "she'd yell and scream. She was in pain."

It took almost 2 1/2 hours for the passers-by, CHP officers, tow truck drivers, and firefighters—about 25 people in all—to secure the car and pull the woman to safety.

"It was kinda funny," L.A. County Fire Capt. Ross Marshall recalled later. "She kept saying, 'I'll do it myself.' "

There are times when self-sufficiency goes too far.

(Self-sufficiency, Help)

Influence 109

In the November 1987 *Reader's Digest,* Betty Wein retells an old tale she heard from Elie Wiesel:

A just man comes to Sodom hoping to save the city. He pickets. What else can he do? He goes from street to street, from marketplace to marketplace, shouting, "Men and women, repent. What you are doing is wrong. It will kill you; it will destroy you."

They laugh, but he goes on shouting, until one day a child stops him. "Poor stranger, don't you see it's useless?"

"Yes," the just man replies.

"Then why do you go on?" the child asks.

"I was convinced that I would change them. Now I go on shouting because I don't want them to change me."

(Testimony, Evil)

Judging others 110

At the turn of the century, the world's most distinguished astronomer was certain there were canals on Mars. Sir Percival Lowell, esteemed for his study of the solar system, had a particular fascination with the Red Planet.

When he heard, in 1877, that an Italian astronomer had seen straight lines crisscrossing the Martian surface, Lowell spent the rest of his years squinting into the eyepiece of his giant telescope in Arizona, mapping the channels and canals he saw. He was convinced the canals were proof of intelligent life on Mars, possibly an older but wiser race than humanity.

Lowell's observations gained wide acceptance. So eminent was he, none dared contradict him.

Now, of course, things are different. Space probes have orbited Mars and landed on its surface. The entire planet has been mapped, and no one has seen a canal. How could Lowell have "seen" so much that wasn't there?

Two possibilities: (1) he so wanted to see canals that he did, over and over again, and (2) we know now that he suffered from a rare eye disease that made him see the blood vessels in his own eyes. The Martian "canals" he saw were nothing more than the bulging veins of his eyeballs. Today the malady is known as "Lowell's syndrome."

When Jesus warns that "in the same way you judge others, you will be judged" and warns of seeing "the speck of sawdust" in another's eye while missing the plank in our own (Matt. 7:1–3), could he not be referring to the spiritual equivalent of Lowell's syndrome? Over and over, we "see" faults in others because we don't want to believe anything better about them. And so often we think we have a firsthand view of their shortcomings, when in fact our vision is distorted by our own disease.

(Criticism, Spiritual perception)

Judging others **111**

The following story appeared in the newsletter *Our America:*

Dodie Gadient, a schoolteacher for thirteen years, decided to travel across America and see the sights she had taught about. Traveling alone in a truck with camper in tow, she launched out. One afternoon rounding a curve on I-5 near Sacramento in rush-hour traffic, a water pump blew on her truck. She was tired, exasperated, scared, and alone. In spite of the traffic jam she caused, no one seemed interested in helping.

Leaning up against the trailer, she prayed, "Please God, send me an angel . . . preferably one with mechanical experience." Within four minutes, a huge Harley drove up, ridden by an enormous man sporting long, black hair, a beard, and tattooed arms. With an incredible air of confidence, he jumped off and, without even glancing at Dodie, went to work on the truck. Within another few minutes, he flagged down a larger truck, attached a tow chain to the frame of the disabled Chevy, and whisked the whole 56-foot rig off the freeway onto a side street, where he calmly continued to work on the water pump.

The intimidated schoolteacher was too dumbfounded to talk. Especially when she read the paralyzing words on the back of his leather jacket: "Hell's Angels—California." As he finished the task, she finally got up the courage to say, "Thanks so much," and carry on a brief conversation.

Noticing her surprise at the whole ordeal, he looked her straight in the eye and mumbled, "Don't judge a book by its cover. You may not know who you're talking to." With that, he smiled, closed the hood of the truck, and straddled his Harley. With a wave, he was gone as fast as he had appeared.

Given half a chance, people often crawl out of the boxes into which we've relegated them.

(Angels, Prayer)

Judgment 112

In *Is It Real When It Doesn't Work?* Doug Murren and Barb Shurin recount:

Toward the end of the nineteenth century, Swedish chemist Alfred Nobel awoke one morning to read his own obituary in the local newspaper: "Alfred Nobel, the inventor of dynamite, who died yesterday, devised a way for more people to be killed in a war than ever before, and he died a very rich man."

Actually, it was Alfred's older brother who had died; a newspaper reporter had bungled the epitaph.

But the account had a profound effect on Nobel. He decided he wanted to be known for something other than developing the means to kill people efficiently and for amassing a fortune in the process. So he initiated the Nobel Prize, the award for scientists and writers who foster peace.

Nobel said, "Every man ought to have the chance to correct his epitaph in midstream and write a new one."

Few things will change us as much as looking at our life as though it is finished.

(Repentance, Death)

Justice 113

Life is unjust. Upon accepting an award, the late Jack Benny once remarked, "I really don't deserve this. But I have arthritis, and I don't deserve that either."

(Suffering, Rights)

Kingdom of God 114

"While serving as a missionary in Laos," tells John Hess-Yoder, "I discovered an illustration of the kingdom of God.

"Before the colonialists imposed national boundaries, the kings of Laos and Vietnam reached an agreement on taxation in the border areas. Those who ate short-grain rice built their houses on stilts, and decorated them with Indian-style serpents were considered Laotians. On the other hand, those who ate long-grain rice, built their houses on the ground, and decorated them with Chinese-style dragons were considered Vietnamese.

"The exact location of a person's home was not what determined his or her nationality. Instead, each person belonged to the kingdom whose cultural values he or she exhibited."

So it is with us: we live in the world, but as part of God's kingdom, we are to live according to his kingdom's standards and values.

(Values, World)

Law 115

Timothy Munyon writes:

While living in Florida, I had several friends who worked cleaning rooms at a nationally known inn located directly on the white sands of the Gulf of Mexico. They spent their work breaks running barefoot in the sand. The problem was the inn required all employees to wear shoes at all times while working.

I noticed the employees responded in one of two ways.

The majority thought the rule restricted their freedom. The rooms had shag carpeting, delightful to bare toes, and just a few steps away lay the beach. To them the rule to wear shoes was nothing more than employer harassment.

But a minority of the employees looked at the rule differently. Sometimes late night parties would produce small pieces of broken glass. Occasionally a stickpin would be found hidden in the deep shag piles. Some knew the pain of skinning bare toes on the steel bed frame while making a bed. This minority saw the rule as protection, not restriction.

Were God's laws written to make life miserable? Or were they written by a loving heavenly Father who cares about his children?

(Freedom, God's love)

In *Who Will Deliver Us?,* Paul F.M. Zahl writes:

A duck hunter was with a friend in the wide-open land of southeastern Georgia. Far away on the horizon he noticed a cloud of smoke. Soon he could hear crackling as the wind shifted. He realized the terrible truth: a brushfire was advancing, so fast they couldn't outrun it.

Rifling through his pockets, he soon found what he was looking for—a book of matches. He lit a small fire around the two of them. Soon they were standing in a circle of blackened earth, waiting for the fire to come.

They didn't have to wait long. They covered their mouths with handkerchiefs and braced themselves. The fire came near—and swept over them. But they were completely unhurt, untouched. Fire would not pass where fire had already passed.

The law is like a brushfire. I cannot escape it. But if I stand in the burned-over place, not a hair of my head will be singed. Christ's death is the burned-over place. There I huddle, hardly believing yet relieved. The law is powerful, yet powerless: Christ's death has disarmed it.

(Atonement, Christ's death)

Leadership 117

In *The Last Days Newsletter,* Leonard Ravenhill tells about a group of tourists visiting a picturesque village who walked by an old man sitting beside a fence. In a rather patronizing way, one tourist asked, "Were any great men born in this village?"

The old man replied, "Nope, only babies."

A frothy question brought a profound answer. There are no instant heroes—whether in this world or in the kingdom of God. Growth takes time, and as 1 Timothy 3:6 and 5:22 point out, even spiritual leadership must be earned.

(Beginnings, Growth)

Leadership 118

Bruce Larson, in his book *Wind and Fire,* points out some interesting facts about sandhill cranes:

These large birds, who fly great distances across continents, have three remarkable qualities. First, they rotate leadership. No one bird stays out in front all the time. Second, they choose leaders who can handle turbulence. And then, all during the time one bird is leading, the rest are honking their affirmation. That's not a bad model for the church. Certainly we need leaders who can handle turbulence and who are aware that leadership ought to be shared. But most of all, we need a church where we are all honking encouragement.

(Encouragement, Church)

Leadership 119

In *Everyday Discipleship for Ordinary People,* Stuart Briscoe writes:

One of my young colleagues was officiating at the funeral of a war veteran. The dead man's military friends wished to have a part in the service at the funeral home, so they requested the pastor to lead them down to the casket, stand with them for a solemn moment of remembrance, and then lead them out through the side door. This he proceeded to do, but unfortunately the effect was somewhat marred when he picked the wrong door. The result was that they marched with military precision into a broom closet, in full view of the mourners, and had to beat a hasty retreat covered with confusion.

This true story illustrates a cardinal rule or two. First, if you're going to lead, make sure you know where you're going. Second, if you're going to follow, make sure that you are following someone who knows what he is doing!

(Followers, Competence)

Some scientists, according to a story by Harold Bredesen, decided to develop a fish that could live outside of water. So, selecting some healthy red herring, they bred and crossbred, hormoned and chromosomed until they produced a fish that could exist out of water.

But the project director wasn't satisfied. He suspected that though the fish had learned to live on dry land, it still had a secret desire for water.

"Re-educate it," he said. "Change its very desires."

So again they went to work, this time retraining even the strongest reflexes. The result? A fish that would rather die than get wet. Even humidity filled this new fish with dread.

The director, proud of his triumph, took the fish on tour. Well, quite accidentally, according to official reports, it happened—the fish fell into a lake. It sank to the bottom, eyes and gills clamped shut, afraid to move, lest it become wetter. And of course it dared not breathe; every instinct said no. Yet breathe it must.

So the fish drew a tentative gill-full. Its eyes bulged. It breathed again and flicked a fin. It breathed a third time and wriggled with delight. Then it darted away. The fish had discovered water.

And with that same wonder, men and women conditioned by a world that rejects God, discover him. For in him we live and move and have our being.

(Rejecting God, Conversion)

Peter W. Law in *A Portrait of My Father* writes:

Imagine you are on holiday, and you have an apartment overlooking the sand and surf. Sitting on the table in your room is a fishbowl, and inside the bowl is a small goldfish. Each day you swim and sun-bake and enjoy soaking up the delights of vacationing. Before long, however, you begin to feel sorry for little Goldie who is all alone in his bowl while you go out having fun in the sun. To make up for this injustice, you promise Goldie a little of the action. "Tomorrow," you tell the goldfish, "you will begin to enjoy life, too."

The next day you take a washcloth, lift the fish from the bowl, place it in the cloth, wrap it up, and put the living bundle into your pocket before leaving for the beach.

As you reach the spot where you are accustomed to spending your day, you can feel the sun's heat beating down upon your back. Excitedly you take your gilled companion from your pocket, lay out the washcloth on the sand, place the fish on the cloth, stand back, and say, "Now this is the life, Goldie; live it up!"

Can anything be more ridiculous or more foolish? Being in the sun on the hot beach is no environment for a goldfish—or any fish! It will die there, not live. It was never intended to be in that environment. For people, a relationship with God as Father is the only correct environment for life.

(Enjoyment, Knowing God)

Light 122

Bob Woods, in *Pulpit Digest,* tells the story of a couple who took their son, 11, and daughter, 7, to Carlsbad Caverns. As always, when the tour reached the deepest point in the cavern, the guide turned off all the lights to dramatize how completely dark and silent it is below the earth's surface.

The little girl, suddenly enveloped in utter darkness, was frightened and began to cry.

Immediately was heard the voice of her brother: "Don't cry. Somebody here knows how to turn on the lights."

In a real sense, that is the message of the gospel: light is available, even when darkness seems overwhelming.

(Darkness, Fear)

Lordship of Christ 123

The captain of the ship looked into the dark night and saw faint lights in the distance. Immediately he told his signalman to send a message: "Alter your course 10 degrees south."

Promptly a return message was received: "Alter your course 10 degrees north."

The captain was angered; his command had been ignored. So he sent a second message: "Alter your course 10 degrees south—I am the captain!"

Soon another message was received: "Alter your course 10 degrees north—I am seaman third class Jones."

Immediately the captain sent a third message, knowing the fear it would evoke: "Alter your course 10 degrees south —I am a battleship."

Then the reply came: "Alter your course 10 degrees north —I am a lighthouse."

In the midst of our dark and foggy times, all sorts of voices are shouting orders into the night, telling us what to do, how to adjust our lives. Out of the darkness, one voice signals something quite opposite to the rest—something almost absurd. But the voice happens to be the Light of the World, and we ignore it at our peril.

(Pride, Submission)

Lostness 124

A novel by Madeleine L'Engle is entitled *A Severed Wasp*. The title, which comes from one of George Orwell's essays, offers a graphic image of human lostness.

Orwell describes a wasp that "was sucking jam on my plate and I cut him in half. He paid no attention, merely went on with his meal, while a tiny stream of jam trickled out of his severed esophagus. Only when he tried to fly away did he grasp the dreadful thing that had happened to him."

The wasp and people without Christ have much in common. Severed from their souls, but greedy and unaware, people continue to consume life's sweetness. Only when it's time to fly away will they grasp their dreadful condition.

(Pleasures, World)

In *The Christian Leader,* Don Ratzlaff retells a story Vernon Grounds came across in Ernest Gordon's *Miracle on the River Kwai.* The Scottish soldiers, forced by their Japanese captors to labor on a jungle railroad, had degenerated to barbarous behavior, but one afternoon something happened:

A shovel was missing. The officer in charge became enraged. He demanded that the missing shovel be produced, or else. When nobody in the squadron budged, the officer got his gun and threatened to kill them all on the spot. . . . It was obvious the officer meant what he had said. Then, finally, one man stepped forward. The officer put away his gun, picked up a shovel, and beat the man to death. When it was over, the survivors picked up the bloody corpse and carried it with them to the second tool check. This time, no shovel was missing. Indeed, there had been a miscount at the first check point.

The word spread like wildfire through the whole camp. An innocent man had been willing to die to save the others! . . . The incident had a profound effect. . . . The men began to treat each other like brothers.

When the victorious Allies swept in, the survivors, human skeletons, lined up in front of their captors . . . (and instead of attacking their captors) insisted: "No more hatred. No more killing. Now what we need is forgiveness."

Sacrificial love has transforming power.

(Forgiveness, Sacrifice)

J. Allan Peterson, in *The Myth of the Greener Grass,* writes:

Newspaper columnist and minister George Crane tells of a wife who came into his office full of hatred toward her husband. "I do not only want to get rid of him; I want to get even. Before I divorce him, I want to hurt him as much as he has me."

Dr. Crane suggested an ingenious plan. "Go home and act as if you really loved your husband. Tell him how much he means to you. Praise him for every decent trait. Go out of your way to be as kind, considerate, and generous as possible. Spare no efforts to please him, to enjoy him. Make him believe you love him. After you've convinced him of your undying love and that you cannot live without him, then drop the bomb. Tell him that you're getting a divorce. That will really hurt him."

With revenge in her eyes, she smiled and exclaimed, "Beautiful, beautiful. Will he ever be surprised!"

And she did it with enthusiasm. Acting "as if." For two months she showed love, kindness, listening, giving, reinforcing, sharing.

When she didn't return, Crane called. "Are you ready now to go through with the divorce?"

"Divorce!" she exclaimed. "Never! I discovered I really do love him." Her actions had changed her feelings. Motion resulted in emotion. The ability to love is established not so much by fervent promise as often repeated deeds.

(Divorce, Marriage)

Love 127

Ian Pitt-Watson adapts this portion from *A Primer for Preachers:*

There is a natural, logical kind of loving that loves lovely things and lovely people. That's logical. But there is another kind of loving that doesn't look for value in what it loves, but that "creates" value in what it loves. Like Rosemary's rag doll.

When Rosemary, my youngest child, was three, she was given a little rag doll, which quickly became an inseparable companion. She had other toys that were intrinsically far more valuable, but none that she loved like she loved the rag doll.

Soon the rag doll became more and more rag and less and less doll. It also became more and more dirty. If you tried to clean the rag doll, it became more ragged still. And if you didn't try to clean the rag doll, it became dirtier still.

The sensible thing to do was to trash the rag doll. But that was unthinkable for anyone who loved my child. If you loved Rosemary, you loved the rag doll—it was part of the package.

"If anyone says, 'I love God' yet hates his brother or sister, he is a liar" (1 John 4:20).

"Love me, love my rag dolls," says God, "including the one you see when you look in the mirror. This is the finest and greatest commandment."

(Church, Unlovable people)

Booker T. Washington was born a slave. Later freed, he headed the Tuskegee Institute and became a leader in education. In his autobiography, he writes:

The most trying ordeal that I was forced to endure as a slave boy . . . was the wearing of a flax shirt. In that portion of Virginia where I lived, it was common to use flax as part of the clothing for the slaves. That part of the flax from which our clothing was made was largely the refuse, which of course was the cheapest and roughest part.

I can scarcely imagine any torture, except, perhaps, the pulling of a tooth, that is equal to that caused by putting on a new flax shirt for the first time. It is almost equal to the feeling that one would experience if he had a dozen or more chestnut burrs, or a hundred small pin-points, in contact with his flesh. . . . But I had no choice, I had to wear the flax shirt or none. . . .

My brother John, who is several years older than I am, performed one of the most generous acts that I have ever heard of one slave relative doing for another. On several occasions when I was being forced to wear a new flax shirt, he generously agreed to put it on in my stead and wear it for several days, till it was "broken in."

(Sacrifice, Help)

Rubel Shelly tells this story:

Jason Tuskes was a 17-year-old high school honor student. He was close to his mother, his wheelchair-bound father, and his younger brother. Jason was an expert swimmer who loved to scuba dive.

He left home on a Tuesday morning to explore a spring and underwater cave near his home in west central Florida. His plan was to be home in time to celebrate his mother's birthday by going out to dinner with his family that night.

Jason became lost in the cave. Then, in his panic, he apparently got wedged into a narrow passageway. When he realized he was trapped, he shed his yellow metal air tank and unsheathed his diver's knife. With the tank as a tablet and the knife as a pen, he wrote one last message to his family: I LOVE YOU MOM, DAD, AND CHRISTIAN. Then he ran out of air and drowned.

A dying message—something communicated in the last few seconds of life—is something we can't ignore. God's final words to us are etched on a Roman cross. They are blood red. They scream to be heard. They, too, say, "I love you."

(God's love, Christ's blood)

Love, for enemies 130

In *Context,* Martin Marty retells a parable from the *Eye of the Needle* newsletter:

A holy man was engaged in his morning meditation under a tree whose roots stretched out over the riverbank. During his meditation he noticed that the river was rising, and a scorpion caught in the roots was about to drown. He crawled out on the roots and reached down to free the scorpion, but every time he did so, the scorpion struck back at him.

An observer came along and said to the holy man, "Don't you know that's a scorpion, and it's in the nature of a scorpion to want to sting?"

To which the holy man replied, "That may well be, but it is my nature to save, and must I change my nature because the scorpion does not change its nature?"

(Evangelism, Perseverance)

Love, for enemies 131

In *The Grace of Giving,* Stephen Olford tells of a Baptist pastor during the American Revolution, Peter Miller, who lived in Ephrata, Pennsylvania, and enjoyed the friendship of George Washington.

In Ephrata also lived Michael Wittman, an evil-minded sort who did all he could to oppose and humiliate the pastor.

One day Michael Wittman was arrested for treason and sentenced to die. Peter Miller traveled seventy miles on foot to Philadelphia to plead for the life of the traitor.

"No, Peter," General Washington said, "I cannot grant you the life of your friend."

"My friend!" exclaimed the old preacher. "He's the bitterest enemy I have."

"What?" cried Washington. "You've walked seventy miles to save the life of an enemy? That puts the matter in a different light. I'll grant your pardon." And he did. Peter Miller took Michael Wittman back home to Ephrata—no longer an enemy, but a friend.

(Grace, Enemies)

Love, for enemies 132

In *The Northwestern Lutheran,* Joel C. Gerlach writes:

Eight times the Ministry of Education in East Germany said no to Uwe Holmer's children when they tried to enroll at the university in East Berlin. The Ministry of Education doesn't usually give reasons for its rejection of applications for enrollment. But in this case the reason wasn't hard to guess.

Uwe Holmer, the father of the eight applicants, is a Lutheran pastor at Lobetal, a suburb of East Berlin. For 26 years the Ministry of Education was headed by Margot Honecker, wife of East Germany's premier, Erich Honecker. . . . [Then] when the Berlin wall cracked . . . Honecker and his wife were unceremoniously dismissed from office. He is now under indictment for criminal activities during his tenure as premier.

At the end of January the Honeckers were evicted from their luxurious palace in Vandlitz, an exclusive suburb of palatial homes reserved for the VIPs in the party. The Honeckers suddenly found themselves friendless, without resources, and with no place to go. None of their former cronies showed them any of the humanitarianism communists boast about. No one wanted to identify with the Honeckers. . . .

Enter Uwe Holmer. Remembering the words of Jesus, "If someone strikes you on the right cheek, turn to him the other also," Holmer extended an invitation to the Honeckers to stay with his family in the parsonage of the parish church in Lobetal. . . .

Pastor Holmer has not reported that the Honeckers have renounced their atheism and professed faith in Jesus as Savior and Lord. But at least they fold their hands and bow their heads when the family prays together. Who knows what the Holmer's faith-in-action plan will lead to before this extraordinary episode ends?

(Enemies, Evangelism)

Loyalty 133

Jackie Robinson was the first black to play major league baseball. While breaking baseball's color barrier, he faced jeering crowds in every stadium.

While playing one day in his home stadium in Brooklyn, he committed an error. His own fans began to ridicule him. He stood at second base, humiliated, while the fans jeered.

Then shortstop "Pee Wee" Reese came over and stood next to him. He put his arm around Jackie Robinson and faced the crowd. The fans grew quiet. Robinson later said that arm around his shoulder saved his career.

(Encouragement, Failure)

Loyalty 134

In the December 31, 1989 *Chicago Tribune,* the editors printed their photos of the decade. One of them, by Michael Fryer, captured a grim fireman and paramedic carrying a fire victim away from the scene.

The blaze, which happened in Chicago in December 1984, at first seemed routine. But then firefighters discovered the bodies of a mother and five children huddled in the kitchen of an apartment.

Fryer said the firefighters surmised, "She could have escaped with two or three of the children but couldn't decide whom to pick. She chose to wait with all of them for the firefighters to arrive. All of them died of smoke inhalation."

There are times when you just don't leave those you love.

(Love, Mothers)

Radio personality Paul Harvey tells the story of how an Eskimo kills a wolf. The account is grisly, yet it offers fresh insight into the consuming, self-destructive nature of sin:

First, the Eskimo coats his knife blade with animal blood and allows it to freeze. Then he adds another layer of blood, and another, until the blade is completely concealed by frozen blood.

Next, the hunter fixes his knife in the ground with the blade up. When a wolf follows his sensitive nose to the source of the scent and discovers the bait, he licks it, tasting the fresh frozen blood. He begins to lick faster, more and more vigorously, lapping the blade until the keen edge is bare. Feverishly now, harder and harder the wolf licks the blade in the arctic night. So great becomes his craving for blood that the wolf does not notice the razor-sharp sting of the naked blade on his own tongue, nor does he recognize the instant at which his insatiable thirst is being satisfied by his "own" warm blood. His carnivorous appetite just craves more—until the dawn finds him dead in the snow!

It is a fearful thing that people can be "consumed by their own lusts."

(Self-destruction, Sin)

Lust 136

In one movie some shipwrecked men are left drifting aimlessly on the ocean in a lifeboat. As the days pass under the scorching sun, their rations of food and fresh water give out. The men grow deliriously thirsty. One night while the others are asleep, one man ignores all previous warnings and gulps down some salt water. He quickly dies.

Ocean water contains seven times more salt than the human body can safely ingest. Drinking it, a person dehydrates because the kidneys demand extra water to flush the overload of salt. The more salt water someone drinks, the thirstier he gets. He actually dies of thirst.

When we lust, we become like this man. We thirst desperately for something that looks like what we want. We don't realize, however, that it is precisely the opposite of what we really need. In fact, it can kill us.

(Thirst, Deception)

A school teacher lost her life savings in a business scheme that had been elaborately explained by a swindler. When her investment disappeared and her dream was shattered, she went to the Better Business Bureau.

"Why on earth didn't you come to us first?" the official asked. "Didn't you know about the Better Business Bureau?"

"Oh, yes," said the lady sadly. "I've always known about you, but I didn't come because I was afraid you'd tell me not to do it."

The folly of human nature is that even though we know where the answers lie—God's Word—we don't turn there for fear of what it will say.

(Bible, God's will)

Marriage 138

A braid appears to contain only two strands of hair. But it is impossible to create a braid with only two strands. If the two could be put together at all, they would quickly unravel.

Herein lies the mystery: What looks like two strands requires a third. The third strand, though not immediately evident, keeps the strands tightly woven.

In a Christian marriage, God's presence, like the third strand in a braid, holds husband and wife together.

(Unity, God's presence)

139

In *On This Day* by Carl D. Windsor, the page for Valentine's Day includes this anecdote:

Even the most devoted couple will experience a stormy bout once in a while. A grandmother, celebrating her golden wedding anniversary, once told the secret of her long and happy marriage. "On my wedding day, I decided to make a list of ten of my husband's faults which, for the sake of our marriage, I would overlook," she said.

A guest asked the woman what some of the faults she had chosen to overlook were. The grandmother replied, "To tell you the truth, my dear, I never did get around to listing them. But whenever my husband did something that made me hopping mad, I would say to myself, *Lucky for him that's one of the ten!*"

(Faultfinding, Forbearance)

Materialism 140

Fortune magazine quotes a comment made by billionaire H. Ross Perot:

"Guys, just remember, if you get real lucky, if you make a lot of money, if you go out and buy a lot of stuff—it's gonna break. You got your biggest, fanciest mansion in the world. It has air conditioning. It's got a pool. Just think of all the pumps that are going to go out. Or go to a yacht basin any place in the world. Nobody is smiling, and I'll tell you why. Something broke that morning. The generator's out; the microwave oven doesn't work. . . . Things just don't mean happiness."

(Treasures, Happiness)

The *Times-Reporter* of New Philadelphia, Ohio, reported in September 1985 a celebration at a New Orleans municipal pool. The party around the pool was held to celebrate the first summer in memory without a drowning at any New Orleans city pool. In honor of the occasion, two hundred people gathered, including one hundred certified lifeguards.

As the party was breaking up and the four lifeguards on duty began to clear the pool, they found a fully dressed body in the deep end. They tried to revive Jerome Moody, thirty-one, but it was too late. He had drowned surrounded by lifeguards celebrating their successful season.

I wonder how many visitors and strangers are among us drowning in loneliness, hurt, and doubt, while we, who could help them, don't realize it. We Christians have reason to celebrate, but our mission, as the old hymn says, is to "rescue the perishing." And often they are right next to us.

(Evangelism, Mission)

Ministry 142

Rusty Stevens, a Navigators director in Virginia Beach, Virginia, tells this story:

As I feverishly pushed the lawn mower around our yard, I wondered if I'd finish before dinner. Mikey, our 6-year-old, walked up and, without even asking, stepped in front of me and placed his hands on the mower handle. Knowing that he wanted to help me, I quit pushing.

The mower quickly slowed to a stop. Chuckling inwardly at his struggles, I resisted the urge to say, "Get out of here, kid. You're in my way," and said instead, "Here, Son. I'll help you." As I resumed pushing, I bowed my back and leaned forward, and walked spread-legged to avoid colliding with Mikey. The grass cutting continued, but more slowly, and less efficiently than before, because Mikey was "helping" me.

Suddenly, tears came to my eyes as it hit me: *This is the way my heavenly Father allows me to "help" him build his kingdom!* I pictured my heavenly Father at work seeking, saving, and transforming the lost, and there I was, with my weak hands "helping." My Father *could* do the work by himself, but he doesn't. He chooses to stoop gracefully to allow me to co-labor with him. Why? For *my* sake, because he wants me to have the privilege of ministering with him.

(Service, Evangelism)

Philip Yancey in *World Concern Update* writes:

I don't know what comes to your mind when you hear the word *fat,* but I have a good idea. In America fat is nearly always a dirty word. We spend billions of dollars on pills, diet books, and exercise machines to help us lose excess fat. I hadn't heard a good word about fat in years—that is, until I met Dr. Paul Brand.

"Fat is absolutely gorgeous," says Brand, a medical doctor who has worked with lepers in India. "When I perform surgery, I marvel at the shimmering, lush layers of fat that spread apart as I open up the body. Those cells insulate against cold, provide protection for the valuable organs underneath, and give a firm, healthy appearance to the whole body." I had never thought of fat quite like that!

"But those are just side benefits," he continues. "The real value of fat is as a storehouse. Locked in those fat cells are the treasures of the human body. When I run or work or expend any energy, fat cells make that possible. They act as banker cells. It's absolutely beautiful to observe the cooperation among those cells!"

Dr. Brand applies the analogy of fat to the body of Christ. Each individual Christian in a relatively wealthy country like America is called to be a fat cell. America has a treasure house of wealth and spiritual resources. The challenge to us, as Christians, is to wisely use those resources for the rest of the body.

Ever since talking to Dr. Brand, I have taken sort of a whimsical pleasure once each month in thinking of myself as a fat cell—on the day I write out checks for Christian organizations. It has helped my attitude. No longer do I concentrate on how I could have used that money I am giving away; rather, I contemplate my privilege to funnel those resources back into Christ's body to help accomplish his work all around the world.

(Stewardship, Body of Christ)

Money 144

In *I Talk Back to the Devil,* A. W. Tozer reminds us:

Money often comes between men and God. Someone has said that you can take two small ten-cent pieces, just two dimes, and shut out the view of a panoramic landscape. Go to the mountains and just hold two coins closely in front of your eyes—the mountains are still there, but you cannot see them at all because there is a dime shutting off the vision in each eye.

It doesn't take large quantities of money to come between us and God; just a little, placed in the wrong position, will effectively obscure our view.

(Spiritual perception, Idolatry)

Many people think money is security, but 1 Timothy 6:9 warns that it can be just the opposite. A few years ago, columnist Jim Bishop reported what happened to people who won the state lottery:

Rosa Grayson of Washington won $400 a week for life. She hides in her apartment. For the first time in her life, she has "nerves." Everyone tries to put the touch on her. "People are so mean," she said. "I hope you win the lottery and see what happens to you."

When the McGugarts of New York won the Irish Sweepstakes, they were happy. Pop was a steamfitter. Johnny, twenty-six, loaded crates on docks. Tim was going to night school. Pop split the million with his sons. They all said the money wouldn't change their plans.

A year later, the million wasn't gone; it was bent. The boys weren't speaking to Pop, or to each other. Johnny was chasing expensive race horses; Tim was catching up with expensive girls. Mom accused Pop of hiding his poke from her. Within two years, all of them were in court for nonpayment of income taxes. "It's the Devil's own money," Mom said. Both boys were studying hard to become alcoholics.

All these people hoped and prayed for sudden wealth. All had their prayers answered. All were wrecked on a dollar sign.

(Coveting, Happiness)

When you go to a doctor for your annual check-up, he or she will often begin to poke, prod, and press various places, all the while asking, "Does this hurt? How about this?"

If you cry out in pain, one of two things has happened. Either the doctor has pushed too hard, without the right sensitivity. Or, more likely, there's something wrong, and the doctor will say, "We'd better do some more tests. It's not supposed to hurt there!"

So it is when pastors preach on financial responsibility, and certain members cry out in discomfort, criticizing the message and the messenger. Either the pastor has pushed too hard, or perhaps there's something wrong. In that case, I say, "My friend, we're in need of the Great Physician because it's not supposed to hurt there."

(Preaching, Stewardship)

Money 147

In *Success, Motivation and the Scriptures* William H. Cook describes a meeting in 1923 of a group of business tycoons. Together these men controlled unthinkable sums of wealth, and for years the media had trumpeted their success stories. On this day in Chicago they assembled to enjoy their mutual success. Dr. Cook relays what happened to these men in the years that followed.

Charles Schwab, the president of the largest independent steel company, lived on borrowed money the last five years of his life and died penniless.

Richard Whitney, the president of the New York Stock Exchange, served time in Sing Sing Prison.

Albert Fall, a former member of the President's Cabinet, was pardoned from prison so he could die at home.

Jesse Livermore, the greatest bear on Wall Street, committed suicide.

Leon Fraser, the president of the Bank of International Settlement, committed suicide.

Ivan Krueger, head of the world's greatest monopoly, committed suicide.

The success they celebrated proved illusory.

(Success, Power)

Morality 148

George Will writes in *Men at Work:*

"Baseball umpires are carved from granite and stuffed with microchips. . . . They are professional dispensers of pure justice. Once when Babe Pinelli called Babe Ruth out on strikes, Ruth made a populist argument. Ruth reasoned fallaciously (as populists do) from raw numbers to moral weight: 'There's 40,000 people here who know that last one was a ball, tomato head.'

"Pinelli replied with the measured stateliness of John Marshall: 'Maybe so, but mine is the only opinion that counts.' "

Christians are also pressed by the weight of numbers aligned against the moral law of God. But the Christian knows that in the end, only one opinion counts: that of the beneficent Umpire of all human affairs.

(Judgment, Opinions)

Mothers 149

John Killinger's book *Lost in Wonder, Love, and Praise* includes the following affirmation:

I believe in Jesus Christ, the Son of the living God,
who was born of the promise to a virgin named Mary.
I believe in the love Mary gave her Son,
that caused her to follow him in his ministry
and stand by his cross as he died.
I believe in the love of all mothers,
and its importance in the lives of the children they bear.
It is stronger than steel, softer than down,
and more resilient than a green sapling on the hillside.
It closes wounds, melts disappointments,
and enables the weakest child to stand tall
and straight in the fields of adversity.
I believe that this love, even at its best,
is only a shadow of the love of God,
a dark reflection of all that we can expect of him,
both in this life and the next.
And I believe that one of the most beautiful sights
in the world is a mother who lets this greater love
flow through her to her child,
blessing the world with the tenderness of her touch
and the tears of her joy.

(Love, Children)

Motives 150

A lady answered the knock on her door to find a man with a sad expression.

"I'm sorry to disturb you," he said, "but I'm collecting money for an unfortunate family in the neighborhood. The husband is out of work, the kids are hungry, the utilities will soon be cut off, and worse, they're going to be kicked out of their apartment if they don't pay the rent by this afternoon."

"I'll be happy to help," said the woman with great concern. "But who are you?"

"I'm the landlord," he replied.

(Mercy, Giving)

Stephen W. Sorenson writes in *Discipleship Journal:*

For two years, because of severe tendinitis in both wrists, I could not pick up my young daughter, carry a log, or even open a twist-off pop bottle. To make matters worse, my wife and I, with help from family and friends, were building a major addition to our home when the tendinitis developed, so I couldn't even use a hammer. I wondered whether I would ever regain full use of my hands.

But our remodeling went on. We installed a second-story window on one blustery evening with the help of some Christian friends and a man named Willie, a retired military musician.

Afterward, before the window crew began eating dinner, I prayed a simple prayer. Willy listened carefully and watched how the rest of us interacted. Later, as he was leaving, he said, "People don't help each other like this anymore."

I replied, "Sure they do!"

Willy came back to our house, day after day. He dug up our septic tank, cut diseased trees, and simply spent time with us. I could sense he understood my pain and our need. One afternoon as he and I walked and talked in the woods, I discovered why.

For most of his life Willy had lived for his music, but a devastating ear problem developed, preventing him from listening to music of any kind. As a result, rather than being put off by my injury, Willy was drawn to me because of our common ground. And before we went separate ways, Willy became a Christian.

As I look back, I don't know if I would have taken time to talk with Willy had my wrists been well. Most likely I'd have been hammering nails or running a chain saw. So "all" I could do was listen and talk. But in God's plan that was enough.

(Help, Evangelism)

Negligence 152

We often fail to consider the gradual, cumulative effect of sin in our lives.

In Saint Louis in 1984, an unemployed cleaning woman noticed a few bees buzzing around the attic of her home. Since there were only a few, she made no effort to deal with them. Over the summer the bees continued to fly in and out the attic vent while the woman remained unconcerned, unaware of the growing city of bees.

The whole attic became a hive, and the ceiling of the second-floor bedroom finally caved in under the weight of hundreds of pounds of honey and thousands of angry bees. While the woman escaped serious injury, she was unable to repair the damage of her accumulated neglect.

(Sin, Problems)

New life 153

The motor home has allowed us to put all the conveniences of home on wheels. A camper no longer needs to contend with sleeping in a sleeping bag, cooking over a fire, or hauling water from a stream. Now he can park a fully equipped home on a cement slab in the midst of a few pine trees and hook up to a water line, a sewer line, and electricity. Some motor homes have a satellite dish attached on top. No more bother with dirt, no more smoke from the fire, no more drudgery of walking to the stream. Now it is possible to go camping and never have to go outside.

We buy a motor home with the hope of seeing new places, of getting out into the world. Yet we deck it out with the same furnishings as in our living room. Thus nothing really changes. We may drive to a new place, set ourselves in new surroundings, but the newness goes unnoticed, for we've only carried along our old setting.

The adventure of new life in Christ begins when the comfortable patterns of the old life are left behind.

(Habits, Change)

Nurture 154

Patients who undergo organ transplants are routinely taken to the intensive care unit after surgery. There they are classified as being in critical but stable condition, even if the operation went well. The doctors and nurses keep a constant watch over them until they become strong enough to be transferred to a less intensive state of care.

New believers in Christ have undergone a serious organ transplant: they have received new hearts. They need careful follow-up and nurture if they are to make it. Leading people to new life in Christ is a cause for celebration. But let's remember they are in critical but stable condition.

(Evangelism, New believers)

Obedience 155

In the eleventh century, King Henry III of Bavaria grew tired of court life and the pressures of being a monarch. He made application to Prior Richard at a local monastery, asking to be accepted as a contemplative and spend the rest of his life in the monastery.

"Your Majesty," said Prior Richard, "do you understand that the pledge here is one of obedience? That will be hard because you have been a king."

"I understand," said Henry. "The rest of my life I will be obedient to you, as Christ leads you."

"Then I will tell you what to do," said Prior Richard. "Go back to your throne and serve faithfully in the place where God has put you."

When King Henry died, a statement was written: "The king learned to rule by being obedient."

When we tire of our roles and responsibilities, it helps to remember God has planted us in a certain place and told us to be a good accountant or teacher or mother or father. Christ expects us to be faithful where he puts us, and when he returns, we'll rule together with him.

(Calling, Faithfulness)

Obedience 156

In *How Life Imitates the World Series,* Dave Bosewell tells a story about Earl Weaver, former manager of the Baltimore Orioles. Sports fans will enjoy how he handled star Reggie Jackson.

Weaver had a rule that no one could steal a base unless given the steal sign. This upset Jackson because he felt he knew the pitchers and catchers well enough to judge who he could and could not steal off of. So one game he decided to steal without a sign. He got a good jump off the pitcher and easily beat the throw to second base. As he shook the dirt off his uniform, Jackson smiled with delight, feeling he had vindicated his judgment to his manager.

Later Weaver took Jackson aside and explained why he hadn't given the steal sign. First, the next batter was Lee May, his best power hitter other than Jackson. When Jackson stole second, first base was left open, so the other team walked May intentionally, taking the bat out of his hands.

Second, the following batter hadn't been strong against that pitcher, so Weaver felt he had to send up a pinch hitter to try to drive in the men on base. That left Weaver without bench strength later in the game when he needed it.

The problem was, Jackson saw only his relationship to the pitcher and catcher. Weaver was watching the whole game.

We, too, see only so far, but God sees the bigger picture. When he sends us a signal, it's wise to obey, no matter what we may think *we* know.

(Trust, God's will)

Obedience 157

In July 1976, Israeli commandos made a daring raid at an airport in Entebbe, Uganda, in which 103 Jewish hostages were freed. In less than 15 minutes, the soldiers had killed all seven of the kidnappers and set the captives free.

As successful as the rescue was, however, three of the hostages were killed during the raid. As the commandos entered the terminal, they shouted in Hebrew, "Get down! Crawl!" The Jewish hostages understood and lay down on the floor, while the guerrillas, who did not speak Hebrew, were left standing. Quickly the rescuers shot the upright kidnappers.

But two of the hostages hesitated—perhaps to see what was happening—and were also cut down. One young man was lying down and actually stood up when the commandos entered the airport. He, too, was shot with the bullets meant for the enemy. Had these three heeded the soldiers' command, they would have been freed with the rest of the captives.

Salvation is open to all, but we must heed Christ's command to repent and make him Lord. Otherwise, we will perish with the judgment meant for the Enemy.

(Judgment, Salvation)

Offerings 158

During his reign, King Frederick William III of Prussia found himself in trouble. Wars had been costly, and in trying to build the nation, he was seriously short of finances. He couldn't disappoint his people, and to capitulate to the enemy was unthinkable.

After careful reflection, he decided to ask the women of Prussia to bring their gold and silver jewelry to be melted down for their country. For each ornament received, he determined to exchange a decoration of bronze or iron as a symbol of his gratitude. Each decoration would be inscribed, "I gave gold for iron, 1813."

The response was overwhelming. Even more important, these women prized their gifts from the king more highly than their former jewelry. The reason, of course, is clear. The decorations were proof that they had sacrificed for their king. Indeed, it became unfashionable to wear jewelry, and thus was established the Order of the Iron Cross. Members wore no ornaments except a cross of iron for all to see.

When Christians come to their King, they too exchange the flourishes of their former life for a cross.

(Sacrifice, Cross)

Joy Davidman in *Smoke on the Mountain,* writes:

Once there was a little old man. His hands trembled; when he ate he clattered the silverware distressingly, missed his mouth with the spoon as often as not, and dribbled a bit of his food on the tablecloth. Now he lived with his married son, having nowhere else to live, and his son's wife didn't like the arrangement.

"I can't have this," she said. "It interferes with my right to happiness." So she and her husband took the old man gently but firmly by the arm and led him to the corner of the kitchen. There they set him on a stool and gave him his food in an earthenware bowl. From then on he always ate in the corner, blinking at the table with wistful eyes.

One day his hands trembled rather more than usual, and the earthenware bowl fell and broke.

"If you are a pig," said the daughter-in-law, "you must eat out of a trough." So they made him a little wooden trough, and he got his meals in that.

These people had a four-year-old son of whom they were very fond. One evening the young man noticed his boy playing intently with some bits of wood and asked what he was doing.

"I'm making a trough," he said, smiling up for approval, "to feed you and Momma out of when I get big."

The man and his wife looked at each other for a while and didn't say anything. Then they cried a little. Then they went to the corner and took the old man by the arm and led him back to the table. They sat him in a comfortable chair and gave him his food on a plate, and from then on nobody ever scolded when he clattered or spilled or broke things.

One of Grimm's fairy tales, this anecdote has the crudity of the old, simple days. But perhaps crudity is what we need to illustrate the naked and crude point of the fifth commandment: honor your parents, lest your children dishonor you. Or, in other words, a society that destroys the family destroys itself.

(Honor, Family)

According to a traditional Hebrew story, Abraham was sitting outside his tent one evening when he saw an old man, weary from age and journey, coming toward him. Abraham rushed out, greeted him, and then invited him into his tent. There he washed the old man's feet and gave him food and drink.

The old man immediately began eating without saying any prayer or blessing. So Abraham asked him, "Don't you worship God?"

The old traveler replied, "I worship fire only and reverence no other god."

When he heard this, Abraham became incensed, grabbed the old man by the shoulders, and threw him out of his tent into the cold night air.

When the old man had departed, God called to his friend Abraham and asked where the stranger was. Abraham replied, "I forced him out because he did not worship you."

God answered, "I have suffered him these eighty years although he dishonors me. Could you not endure him one night?"

(Evangelism, Unbelievers)

Richard Dunagin writes:

At their school carnival our kids won four free goldfish (lucky us!), so out I went Saturday morning to find an aquarium.

The first few I priced ranged from forty to seventy dollars. Then I spotted it—right in the aisle: a discarded ten-gallon display tank, complete with gravel and filter—for a mere five bucks. Sold! Of course, it was nasty dirty, but the savings made the two hours of clean-up a breeze.

Those four new fish looked great in their new home, at least for the first day. But by Sunday one had died. Too bad, but three remained. Monday morning revealed a second casualty, and by Monday night a third goldfish had gone belly up.

We called in an expert member of our church who has a thirty-gallon tank. It didn't take him long to discover the problem: I had washed the tank with soap, an absolute no-no. My uninformed efforts had destroyed the very lives I was trying to protect.

Sometimes in our zeal to clean up our own lives or the lives of others, we unfortunately use "killer soaps"—condemnation, criticism, nagging, fits of temper. We think we're doing right, but our harsh, self-righteous treatment is more than others can bear.

(Self-righteousness, Criticism)

Patience 162

Some years ago a speedboat driver who had survived a racing accident described what had happened. He said he had been at near top speeds when his boat veered slightly and hit a wave at a dangerous angle. The combined force of his speed and the size and angle of the wave sent the boat spinning crazily into the air. He was thrown from his seat and propelled deeply into the water—so deep, in fact, that he had no idea which direction the surface was. He had to remain calm and wait for the buoyancy of his life vest to begin pulling him up. Once he discovered which way was up, he could swim for the surface.

Sometimes we find ourselves surrounded by confusing options, too deeply immersed in our problems to know which way is up. When this happens, we too can remain calm, waiting for God's gentle tug to pull us in the proper direction. Our "life vest" may be other Christians, Scripture, or some other leading from the Holy Spirit, but the key is recognizing our dependency upon God and trusting him.

(Direction, God's will)

Perseverance 163

On opening day of the 1954 baseball season, the Milwaukee Braves visited the Cincinnati Reds. Two rookies began their major league careers with that game. The Reds won 9-8 as Jim Greengrass hit four doubles in his first big-league game. A sensational debut for a young player with a made-for-baseball name!

The rookie starting in left field for the Braves went 0 for 5. Not a very auspicious start for one Henry Aaron.

(Failure, Spiritual gifts)

Perseverance 164

During a Monday night football game between the Chicago Bears and the New York Giants, one of the announcers observed that Walter Payton, the Bears' running back, had accumulated over nine miles in career rushing yardage. The other announcer remarked, "Yeah, and that's with someone knocking him down every 4.6 yards!"

Walter Payton, the most successful running back ever, knows that everyone—even the best—gets knocked down. The key to success is to get up and run again just as hard.

(Obstacles, Success)

Perseverance 165

John Killinger retells this story from *Atlantic Monthly* about the days of the great western cattle ranches:

A little burro sometimes would be harnessed to a wild steed. Bucking and raging, convulsing like drunken sailors, the two would be turned loose like Laurel and Hardy to proceed out onto the desert range. They could be seen disappearing over the horizon, the great steed dragging that little burro along and throwing him about like a bag of cream puffs. They might be gone for days, but eventually they would come back. The little burro would be seen first, trotting back across the horizon, leading the submissive steed in tow. Somewhere out there on the rim of the world, that steed would become exhausted from trying to get rid of the burro, and in that moment, the burro would take mastery and become the leader.

And that's the way it is with the kingdom and its heroes, isn't it? The battle goes to the determined, not to the outraged; to the committed, not to those who are merely dramatic.

(Determination, Emotions)

Perseverance 166

On March 6, 1987, Eamon Coughlan, the Irish world record holder at 1500 meters, was running in a qualifying heat at the World Indoor Track Championships in Indianapolis. With two and a half laps left, he was tripped. He fell, but he got up and with great effort managed to catch the leaders. With only 20 yards left in the race, he was in third place—good enough to qualify for the finals.

He looked over his shoulder to the inside, and, seeing no one, he let up. But another runner, charging hard on the outside, passed Coughlan a yard before the finish, thus eliminating him from the finals. Coughlan's great comeback effort was rendered worthless by taking his eyes off the finish line.

It's tempting to let up when the sights around us look favorable. But we finish well in the Christian race only when we fix our eyes on the goal: Jesus Christ.

(Focus, Zeal)

Perspective 167

Fraiser of Lisuland in northern Burma translated the Scriptures into the Lisu language and then left a young fellow with the task of teaching the people to read.

When he returned six months later, he found three students and the teacher seated around a table, with the Scriptures opened in front of the teacher. When the students each read, they left the Bible where it was. The man on the left read it sideways, the man on the right read it sideways but from the other side, and the man across from the teacher read it upside down. Since they always occupied the same chairs, that's how each had learned to read, and that's how each thought the language was written.

We, too, can be like that. When we learn something from only one perspective, we may think it's the only perspective. Sometimes it's good to change seats to assume a different perspective on the same truth.

(Conviction, Truth)

Dr. George Sweeting wrote in *Special Sermons for Special Days:*

Several years ago our family visited Niagara Falls. It was spring, and ice was rushing down the river. As I viewed the large blocks of ice flowing toward the falls, I could see that there were carcasses of dead fish embedded in the ice. Gulls by the score were riding down the river feeding on the fish. As they came to the brink of the falls, their wings would go out, and they would escape from the falls.

I watched one gull which seemed to delay and wondered when it would leave. It was engrossed in the carcass of a fish, and when it finally came to the brink of the falls, out went its powerful wings. The bird flapped and flapped and even lifted the ice out of the water, and I thought it would escape. But it had delayed too long so that its claws had frozen into the ice. The weight of the ice was too great, and the gull plunged into the abyss.

The finest attractions of this world become deadly when we become overly attached to them. They may take us to our destruction if we cannot give them up. And as Sweeting observed, "Oh, the danger of delay!"

(Repentance, Sin)

Power 169

One New Year's Day, in the Tournament of Roses parade, a beautiful float suddenly sputtered and quit. It was out of gas. The whole parade was held up until someone could get a can of gas.

The amusing thing was this float represented the Standard Oil Company. With its vast oil resources, its truck was out of gas.

Often, Christians neglect their spiritual maintenance, and though they are "clothed with power" (Luke 24:49) find themselves out of gas.

(Holy Spirit, Devotional life)

Power 170

In a seminary missions class, Herbert Jackson told how, as a new missionary, he was assigned a car that would not start without a push.

After pondering his problem, he devised a plan. He went to the school near his home, got permission to take some children out of class, and had them push his car off. As he made his rounds, he would either park on a hill or leave his car running. He used this ingenious procedure for two years.

Ill health forced the Jackson family to leave, and a new missionary came to that station. When Jackson proudly began to explain his arrangement for getting the car started, the new man began looking under the hood. Before the explanation was complete, the new missionary interrupted, "Why Dr. Jackson, I believe the only trouble is this loose cable." He gave the cable a twist, stepped into the car, pushed the switch, and to Jackson's astonishment, the engine roared to life.

For two years needless trouble had become routine. The power was there all the time. Only a loose connection kept Jackson from putting the power to work.

J. B. Phillips paraphrases Ephesians 1:19-20, "How tremendous is the power available to us who believe in God." When we make firm our connection with God, his life and power flow through us.

(Prayer, Self-reliance)

Prayer 171

They tell us the 911 emergency system is the state of the art. All you need do is dial those numbers, and you will almost instantly be connected to a dispatcher. In front of the dispatcher will be a read-out that lists your telephone number, your address, and the name by which that telephone number is listed at that address. Also listening in are the police, the fire department, and the paramedics.

A caller might not be able to say what the problem is. Or perhaps a woman's husband has just suffered a heart attack, and she is so out of control that all she can do is hysterically scream into the telephone. But the dispatcher doesn't need her to say anything. He knows where the call is coming from. Help is already on the way.

There come times in our lives when in our desperation and pain we dial 911 prayers. Sometimes we're hysterical. Sometimes we don't know the words to speak. But God hears. He knows our name and our circumstance. Help is on the way; God has already begun to bring the remedy.

(Crisis, Help)

In a recent issue of *GLASS Window*, a contributor recalls that several years ago, *The British Weekly* published this provocative letter:

> Dear Sir:
>
> It seems ministers feel their sermons are very important and spend a great deal of time preparing them. I have been attending church quite regularly for thirty years, and I have probably heard 3,000 of them. To my consternation, I discovered I cannot remember a single sermon. I wonder if a minister's time might be more profitably spent on something else?

For weeks a storm of editorial responses ensued . . . finally ended by this letter:

> Dear Sir:
>
> I have been married for thirty years. During that time I have eaten 32,850 meals—mostly my wife's cooking. Suddenly I have discovered I cannot remember the menu of a single meal. And yet . . . I have the distinct impression that without them, I would have starved to death long ago.

(Scripture, Church attendance)

Pride 173

Pride is the dandelion of the soul. Its root goes deep; only a little left behind sprouts again. Its seeds lodge in the tiniest encouraging cracks. And it flourishes in good soil: The danger of pride is that it feeds on goodness.

(Goodness, Humility)

Priorities 174

Film maker Walt Disney was ruthless in cutting anything that got in the way of a story's pacing. Ward Kimball, one of the animators for *Snow White*, recalls working 240 days on a 4-1/2 minute sequence in which the dwarfs made soup for Snow White and almost destroyed the kitchen in the process. Disney thought it was funny, but he decided the scene stopped the flow of the picture, so out it went.

When the film of our lives is shown, will it be as great as it might be? A lot will depend on the multitude of 'good' things we need to eliminate to make way for the great things God wants to do through us.

(Sacrifice, Excellence)

Priorities 175

Ben Patterson writes in *The Grand Essentials:*

I have a theory about old age. . . . I believe that when life has whittled us down, when joints have failed and skin has wrinkled and capillaries have clogged and hardened, what is left of us will be what we were all along, in our essence.

Exhibit A is a distant uncle. . . . All his life he did nothing but find new ways to get rich. . . . He spent his senescence very comfortably, drooling and babbling constantly about the money he had made. . . . When life whittled him down to his essence, all there was left was raw greed. This is what he had cultivated in a thousand little ways over a lifetime.

Exhibit B is my wife's grandmother. . . . When she died in her mid-eighties, she had already been senile for several years. What did this lady talk about? The best example I can think of was when we asked her to pray before dinner. She would reach out and hold the hands of those sitting beside her, a broad, beatific smile would spread across her face, her dim eyes would fill with tears as she looked up to heaven, and her chin would quaver as she poured out her love to Jesus. That was Edna in a nutshell. She loved Jesus and she loved people. She couldn't remember our names, but she couldn't keep her hands from patting us lovingly whenever we got near her.

When life whittled her down to her essence, all there was left was love: love for God and love for people.

(Love, Aging)

Priorities 176

It was a 99° September day in San Antonio, when a 10-month-old baby girl was accidently locked inside a parked car by her aunt. Frantically the mother and aunt ran around the auto in near hysteria, while a neighbor attempted to unlock the car with a clothes hanger. Soon the infant was turning purple and had foam on her mouth.

It had become a life-or-death situation when Fred Arriola, a wrecker driver, arrived on the scene. He grabbed a hammer and smashed the back window of the car to set her free.

Was he heralded a hero? "The lady was mad at me because I broke the window," Arriola reported. "I just thought, *What's more important—the baby or the window?*"

Most questions of priority are not between something important and something trivial; rather, between the important and the most important.

(Choices, Wisdom)

Problems 177

One of the classic baseball television shots comes from the 1975 World Series, in which NBC captured Carlton Fisk, jumping up and down, waving his arms, trying to coax his hit to stay fair. It did—for a home run.

That colorful close-up would have been missed had the cameraman followed the ball with his camera, as was his responsibility. But the cameraman inside the Fenway Park scoreboard had one eye on a rat that was circling him. So instead of focusing the camera on the ball, he left it on Fisk.

Sometimes we encounter problems like that rat. We have no idea how they will be resolved, but because of them, we may see God work in a way we never would have without the problems.

(Trust, Trials)

Promises 178

Booker T. Washington describes meeting an ex-slave from Virginia in his book *Up from Slavery:*

I found that this man had made a contract with his master, two or three years previous to the Emancipation Proclamation, to the effect that the slave was to be permitted to buy himself, by paying so much per year for his body; and while he was paying for himself, he was to be permitted to labor where and for whom he pleased.

Finding that he could secure better wages in Ohio, he went there. When freedom came, he was still in debt to his master some 300 dollars. Notwithstanding that the Emancipation Proclamation freed him from any obligation to his master, this black man walked the greater portion of the distance back to where his old master lived in Virginia, and placed the last dollar, with interest, in his hands.

In talking to me about this, the man told me that he knew that he did not have to pay his debt, but that he had given his word to his master, and his word he had never broken. He felt that he could not enjoy his freedom till he had fulfilled his promise.

(Debts, Money)

Recognition 179

Every young student knows of Isaac Newton's famed encounter with a falling apple. Newton discovered and introduced the laws of gravity in the 1600s, which revolutionized astronomical studies.

But few know that if it weren't for Edmund Halley, the world might never have learned from Newton.

It was Halley who challenged Newton to think through his original notions. Halley corrected Newton's mathematical errors and prepared geometrical figures to support his discoveries. Halley coaxed the hesitant Newton to write his great work, *Mathematical Principles of Natural Philosophy*. Halley edited and supervised the publication, and actually financed its printing even though Newton was wealthier and easily could have afforded the printing costs.

Historians call it one of the most selfless examples in the annals of science. Newton began almost immediately to reap the rewards of prominence; Halley received little credit.

He did use the principles to predict the orbit and return of the comet that would later bear his name, but only *after* his death did he receive any acclaim. And because the comet only returns every seventy-six years, the notice is rather infrequent. Halley remained a devoted scientist who didn't care who received the credit as long as the cause was being advanced.

Others have played Halley's role. John the Baptist said of Jesus, "He must become greater; I must become less." Barnabas was content to introduce others to greatness. Many pray to uphold the work of one Christian leader. Such selflessness advances the kingdom.

(Selflessness, Body of Christ)

Rejection 180

Campbell Morgan was one of 150 young men who sought entrance to the Wesleyan ministry in 1888. He passed the doctrinal examinations, but then faced the trial sermon. In a cavernous auditorium that could seat more than 1,000 sat three ministers and 75 others who came to listen.

When Morgan stepped into the pulpit, the vast room and the searching, critical eyes caught him up short. Two weeks later Morgan's name appeared among the 105 rejected for the ministry that year.

Jill Morgan, his daughter-in-law, wrote in her book, *A Man of the Word*: "He wired to his father the one word, 'Rejected,' and sat down to write in his diary: 'Very dark everything seems. Still, He knoweth best.'

"Quickly came the reply: 'Rejected on earth. Accepted in Heaven. Dad.' "

Rejection is rarely permanent, as Morgan went on to prove. Even in this life, circumstances change, and ultimately, there is no rejection of those accepted by Christ.

(Failure, Acceptance)

Repentance 181

When Michigan played Wisconsin in basketball early in the season in 1989, Michigan's Rumeal Robinson stepped to the foul line for two shots late in the fourth quarter. His team trailed by one point, so Rumeal could regain the lead for Michigan. He missed both shots, allowing Wisconsin to upset favored Michigan.

Rumeal felt awful about costing his team the game, but his sorrow didn't stop at the emotional level. After each practice for the rest of the season, Rumeal shot 100 extra foul shots.

Thus, Rumeal was ready when he stepped to the foul line to shoot two shots with three seconds left in overtime in the national championship game. Swish went the first shot, and swish went the second. Those shots won Michigan the national championship.

Rumeal's repentance had been genuine, and sorrow motivated him to work so that he would never make that mistake again. As Paul wrote, "Godly sorrow leads to repentance" (2 Cor. 7:10).

(Failure, Work)

Repentance 182

Paul Lee Tan's *Encyclopedia of 7,700 Illustrations* records:

The Romans sometimes compelled a captive to be joined face-to-face with a dead body, and to bear it about until the horrible effluvia destroyed the life of the living victim. Virgil describes this cruel punishment:

"The living and the dead at his command
were coupled face to face, and hand to hand;
Till choked with stench, in loathed embraces tied,
The lingering wretches pined away and died."

Without Christ, we are shackled to a dead corpse—our sinfulness. Only repentance frees us from certain death, for life and death cannot coexist indefinitely.

(Sin, Life)

Revenge 183

In Judith Viorst's children's book *I'll Fix Anthony*, the younger brother complains about the way his older brother Anthony treats him:

My brother Anthony can read books now, but he won't read any books to me. He plays checkers with Bruce from his school. But when I want to play he says "Go away or I'll clobber you." I let him wear my Snoopy sweatshirt, but he never lets me borrow his sword. Mother says deep down in his heart Anthony loves me. Anthony says deep down in his heart he thinks I stink. Mother says deep deep down in his heart, where he doesn't even know it, Anthony loves me. Anthony says deep deep down in his heart he still thinks I stink. When I'm six, I'll fix Anthony. . . .

When I'm six, I'll float, but Anthony will sink to the bottom. I'll dive off the board, but Anthony will change his mind. I'll breathe in and out when I should, but Anthony will only go glug, glug. . . . When I'm six my teeth will fall out, and I'll put them under the bed, and the tooth fairy will take them away and leave dimes. Anthony's teeth won't fall out. He'll wiggle and wiggle them, but they won't fall out. I might sell him one of my teeth, but I might not. . . .

Anthony is chasing me out of the playroom. He says I stink. He says he is going to clobber me. I have to run now, but I won't have to run when I'm six. When I'm six, I'll fix Anthony.

Most of us know the feeling of Anthony's brother. The Bible calls it revenge.

(Hatred, Forgiveness)

Rewards 184

Robert De Moor, in *The Banner,* writes:

The parable of the vineyard workers (Matt. 20) offends our sense of fairness. Why should everyone get equal pay for unequal work?

Back in Ontario when the apples ripened, Mom would sit all seven of us down, Dad included, with pans and paring knives until the mountain of fruit was reduced to neat rows of filled canning jars. She never bothered keeping track of how many we did, though the younger ones undoubtedly proved more of a nuisance than a help: cut fingers, squabbles over who got which pan, apple core fights. But when the job was done, the reward for everyone was the same: the largest chocolate dipped cone money could buy. A stickler might argue it wasn't quite fair since the older ones actually peeled apples. But I can't remember anyone complaining about it.

A family understands it operates under a different set of norms than a courtroom. In fact, when the store ran out of ice cream and my younger brother had to make do with a Popsicle, we felt sorry for him despite his lack of productivity (he'd eaten all the apples he'd peeled that day—both of them).

God wants all his children to enjoy the complete fullness of eternal life. No true child of God wants it any other way.

(Family, Fairness)

Rewards 185

Ray Stedman in *Talking to My Father*, writes:

An old missionary couple had been working in Africa for years, and they were returning to New York City to retire. They had no pension; their health was broken; they were defeated, discouraged, and afraid. They discovered they were booked on the same ship as President Teddy Roosevelt, who was returning from one of his big-game hunting expeditions.

No one paid attention to them. They watched the fanfare that accompanied the President's entourage, with passengers trying to catch a glimpse of the great man.

As the ship moved across the ocean, the old missionary said to his wife, "Something is wrong. Why should we have given our lives in faithful service for God in Africa all these many years and have no one care a thing about us? Here this man comes back from a hunting trip and everybody makes much over him, but nobody gives two hoots about us."

"Dear, you shouldn't feel that way," his wife said.

"I can't help it; it doesn't seem right."

When the ship docked in New York, a band was waiting to greet the President. The mayor and other dignitaries were there. The papers were full of the President's arrival, but no one noticed this missionary couple. They slipped off the ship and found a cheap flat on the East side, hoping the next day to see what they could do to make a living in the city.

That night the man's spirit broke. He said to his wife, "I can't take this; God is not treating us fairly."

His wife replied, "Why don't you go in the bedroom and tell that to the Lord?"

A short time later he came out from the bedroom, but now his face was completely different. His wife asked, "Dear, what happened?"

"The Lord settled it with me," he said. "I told him how bitter I was that the President should receive this tremendous homecoming, when *no one* met us as we returned home. And when I finished, it seemed as though the Lord put his hand on my shoulder and simply said, '*But you're not home yet!*' "

Yes, there *are* rewards for faithfulness, but not necessarily down here.

(Faithfulness, Heaven)

Righteousness 186

In the Antarctic summer of 1908-9, Sir Ernest Shackleton and three companions attempted to travel to the South Pole from their winter quarters. They set off with four ponies to help carry the load. Weeks later, their ponies dead, rations all but exhausted, they turned back toward their base, their goal not accomplished. Altogether, they trekked 127 days.

On the return journey, as Shackleton records in *The Heart of the Antarctic*, the time was spent talking about food —elaborate feasts, gourmet delights, sumptuous menus. As they staggered along, suffering from dysentery, not knowing whether they would survive, every waking hour was occupied with thoughts of eating.

Jesus, who also knew the ravages of food deprivation, said, "Blessed are those who hunger and thirst for *righteousness*." We can understand Shackleton's obsession with food, which offers a glimpse of the passion Jesus intends for our quest for righteousness.

(Hunger, Scripture)

Fred Craddock, in an address to ministers, caught the practical implications of consecration:

To give my life for Christ appears glorious. To pour myself out for others . . . to pay the ultimate price of martyrdom—I'll do it. I'm ready, Lord, to go out in a blaze of glory.

We think giving our all to the Lord is like taking a $1,000 bill and laying it on the table—"Here's my life, Lord. I'm giving it all."

But the reality for most of us is that he sends us to the bank and has us cash in the $1,000 for quarters. We go through life putting out 25 cents here and 50 cents there. Listen to the neighbor kid's troubles instead of saying, "Get lost." Go to a committee meeting. Give a cup of water to a shaky old man in a nursing home.

Usually giving our life to Christ isn't glorious. It's done in all those little acts of love, 25 cents at a time. It would be easy to go out in a flash of glory; it's harder to live the Christian life little by little over the long haul.

(Consecration, Little things)

Sacrifice 188

In *Christian Living*, Lafcadio Hearn tells of a Japanese seashore village over a hundred years ago, where an earthquake startled the villagers one autumn evening. But, being accustomed to earthquakes, they soon went back to their activities. Above the village on a high plain, an old farmer was watching from his house. He looked at the sea, and the water appeared dark and acted strangely, moving against the wind, running away from the land. The old man knew what it meant. His one thought was to warn the people in the village.

He called to his grandson, "Bring me a torch! Make haste!" In the fields behind him lay his great crop of rice. Piled in stacks ready for the market, it was worth a fortune. The old man hurried out with his torch. In a moment the dry stalks were blazing. Then the big bell pealed from the temple below: Fire!

Back from the beach, away from the strange sea, up the steep side of the cliff, came the people of the village. They were coming to try to save the crops of their rich neighbor. "He's mad!" they said.

As they reached the plain, the old man shouted back at the top of his voice, "Look!" At the edge of the horizon they saw a long, lean, dim line—a line that thickened as they gazed. That line was the sea, rising like a high wall and coming more swiftly than a kite flies. Then came a shock, heavier than thunder. The great swell struck the shore with a weight that sent a shudder through the hills and tore their homes to matchsticks. It drew back, roaring. Then it struck again, and again, and yet again. Once more it struck and ebbed; then it returned to its place.

On the plain no word was spoken. Then the voice of the old man was heard, saying gently, "That is why I set fire to the rice." He stood among them almost as poor as the poorest, for his wealth was gone—but he had saved 400 lives by the sacrifice.

(Love, Giving)

Joseph Ton was pastor of Second Baptist Church, Oradea, Rumania, until he was exiled by the Rumanian government in 1981. In *Pastoral Renewal*, he writes of his experience:

"Years ago I ran away from my country to study theology at Oxford. In 1972, when I was ready to go back to Rumania, I discussed my plans with some fellow students. They pointed out that I might be arrested at the border. One student asked, 'Joseph, what chances do you have of successfully implementing your plans?' "

Ton asked God about it, and God brought to mind Matthew 10:16—"I send you as sheep in the midst of wolves"—and seemed to say, "Tell me, what chance does a sheep surrounded by wolves have of surviving five minutes, let alone of converting the wolves? Joseph, that's how I send you: totally defenseless and without a reasonable hope of success. If you are willing to go like that, go. If you are not willing to be in that position, don't go."

Ton writes: "After our return, as I preached uninhibitedly, harassment and arrests came. One day during interrogation an officer threatened to kill me. Then I said, 'Sir, your supreme weapon is killing. My supreme weapon is dying. Sir, you know my sermons are all over the country on tapes now. If you kill me, I will be sprinkling them with my blood. Whoever listens to them after that will say, "I'd better listen. This man sealed it with his blood." They will speak ten times louder than before. So, go on and kill me. I win the supreme victory then.' "

The officer sent him home. "That gave me pause. For years I was a Christian who was cautious because I wanted to survive. I had accepted all the restrictions the authorities put on me because I wanted to live. Now I wanted to die, and they wouldn't oblige. Now I could do whatever I wanted in Rumania. For years I wanted to save my life, and I was losing it. Now that I wanted to lose it, I was winning it."

(Martyrs, Fear)

Salvation 190

The following drama was originally reported by Peter Michelmore in the October 1987 *Reader's Digest*:

Normally the flight from Nassau to Miami took Walter Wyatt, Jr., only sixty-five minutes. But on December 5, 1986, he attempted it after thieves had looted the navigational equipment in his Beechcraft. With only a compass and a hand-held radio, Walter flew into skies blackened by storm clouds.

When his compass began to gyrate, Walter concluded he was headed in the wrong direction. He flew his plane below the clouds, hoping to spot something, but soon he knew he was lost. He put out a mayday call, which brought a Coast Guard Falcon search plane to lead him to an emergency landing strip only six miles away.

Suddenly Wyatt's right engine coughed its last and died. The fuel tank had run dry. Around 8 P.M. Wyatt could do little more than glide the plane into the water. Wyatt survived the crash, but his plane disappeared quickly, leaving him bobbing on the water in a leaky life vest.

With blood on his forehead, Wyatt floated on his back. Suddenly he felt a hard bump against his body. A shark had found him. Wyatt kicked the intruder and wondered if he would survive the night. He managed to stay afloat for the next ten hours.

In the morning, Wyatt saw no airplanes, but in the water a dorsal fin was headed for him. Twisting, he felt the hide of a shark brush against him. In a moment, two more bull sharks sliced through the water toward him. Again he kicked the sharks, and they veered away, but he was nearing exhaustion.

Then he heard the hum of a distant aircraft. When it was within a half mile, he waved his orange vest. The pilot dropped a smoke canister and radioed the cutter Cape York, which was twelve minutes away: "Get moving, cutter! There's a shark targeting this guy!"

As the Cape York pulled alongside Wyatt, a Jacob's ladder was dropped over the side. Wyatt climbed wearily out of the water and onto the ship, where he fell to his knees and kissed the deck.

He'd been saved. He didn't need encouragement or better techniques. Nothing less than outside intervention could have rescued him from sure death. How much we are like Walter Wyatt!

(Christ, Self-help)

In January 1985, a large suitcase, unmarked and unclaimed, was discovered at the customs office at Los Angeles International Airport. When U.S. Customs agents opened the suitcase, they found the curled-up body of an unidentified young woman.

She had been dead for a few days, according to the county coroner. As the investigation continued, it was learned that the woman was the wife of a young Iranian living in the U.S. Unable to obtain a visa to enter the U.S. and join her husband, she took matters into her own hands and attempted to smuggle herself into America via an airplane's cargo bay. While her plan seemed to her simple though risky, officials were hard pressed to understand how such an attempt could ever succeed. Even if she survived the journey in the cargo bay, she would remain an illegal alien, having entered through improper channels.

Some people believe they'll enter the kingdom of God on their own since they've been reasonably good citizens or church attenders. But entry plans of our own design prove not only foolish but fatal.

(Good works, Kingdom of God)

In 1818, Ignaz Phillip Semmelweis was born into a world of dying women. The finest hospitals lost one out of six young mothers to the scourge of "childbed fever."

A doctor's daily routine began in the dissecting room where he performed autopsies. From there he made his way to the hospital to examine expectant mothers without ever pausing to wash his hands. Dr. Semmelweis was the first man in history to associate such examinations with the resultant infection and death. His own practice was to wash with a chlorine solution, and after eleven years and the delivery of 8,537 babies, he lost only 184 mothers—about one in fifty.

He spent the vigor of his life lecturing and debating with his colleagues. Once he argued, "Puerperal fever is caused by decomposed material conveyed to a wound. . . . I have shown how it can be prevented. I have proved all that I have said. But while we talk, talk, talk, gentlemen, women are dying. I am not asking anything world shaking. I am asking you only to wash. . . . For God's sake, wash your hands."

But virtually no one believed him. Doctors and midwives had been delivering babies for thousands of years without washing, and no outspoken Hungarian was going to change them now! Semmelweis died insane at the age of 47, his wash basins discarded, his colleagues laughing in his face, and the death rattle of a thousand women ringing in his ears.

"Wash me!" was the anguished prayer of King David. "Wash!" was the message of John the Baptist. "Unless I wash you, you have no part with me," said the towel-draped Jesus to Peter. Without our being washed clean, we all die from the contamination of sin. For God's sake, wash!

(Sin, Custom)

In 1981, a Minnesota radio station reported a story about a stolen car in California. Police were staging an intense search for the vehicle and the driver, even to the point of placing announcements on local radio stations to contact the thief.

On the front seat of the stolen car sat a box of crackers that, unknown to the thief, were laced with poison. The car owner had intended to use the crackers as rat bait. Now the police and the owner of the VW Bug were more interested in apprehending the thief to save his life than to recover the car.

So often when we run from God, we feel it is to escape his punishment. But what we are actually doing is eluding his rescue.

(Fear of God, Running from God)

Sanctification 194

The Australian coat of arms pictures two creatures—the emu, a flightless bird, and the kangaroo. The animals were chosen because they share a characteristic that appealed to the Australian citizens. Both the emu and the kangaroo can move only forward, not back. The emu's three-toed foot causes it to fall if it tries to go backwards, and the kangaroo is prevented from moving in reverse by its large tail.

Those who truly choose to follow Jesus become like the emu and kangaroo, moving only forward, never back (Luke 9:62).

(Vision, Progress)

Second coming 195

In the 1987 NCAA Regional Finals, LSU was leading Indiana by eight points with only a few minutes left in the game. As is often the case with a team in the lead, LSU began playing a different ball game. The television announcer pointed out that the LSU players were beginning to watch the clock rather than wholeheartedly play the game. As a result of this shift in focus, Indiana closed the gap, won the game by one point, and eventually went on to become NCAA champions.

While Jesus called us to be aware of "the signs of the times," he clearly called us to expend our energies in faithful, active service. As we await Jesus' promised return, we are not so much to watch the clock as to be diligent servants during the time we have available.

(Service, Signs of the times)

Missionary Gregory Fisher writes:

"What will he say when he shouts?"

The question took me by surprise. I had already found that West African Bible College Students can ask some of the most penetrating questions about minute details of Scripture.

"Reverend, 1 Thessalonians 4:16 says that Christ will descend from heaven with a loud command. I would like to know what that command will be."

I wanted to leave the question unanswered, to tell him that we must not go past what Scripture has revealed, but my mind wandered to an encounter I had earlier in the day with a refugee from the Liberian civil war.

The man, a high school principal, told me how he was apprehended by a two-man death squad. After several hours of terror, as the men described how they would torture and kill him, he narrowly escaped. After hiding in the bush for two days, he was able to find his family and escape to a neighboring country. The escape cost him dearly: two of his children lost their lives. The stark cruelty unleashed on an unsuspecting, undeserving population had touched me deeply.

I also saw flashbacks of the beggars that I pass each morning on my way to the office. Every day I see how poverty destroys dignity, robs men of the best of what it means to be human, and sometimes substitutes the worst of what it means to be an animal. I am haunted by the vacant eyes of people who have lost all hope.

"Reverend, you have not given me an answer. What will he say?"

The question hadn't gone away. " '*Enough,*' " I said "He will shout, 'Enough!' when he returns."

A look of surprise opened the face of the student. "What do you mean, 'enough'?"

"Enough suffering. Enough starvation. Enough terror. Enough death. Enough indignity. Enough lives trapped in hopelessness. Enough sickness and disease. Enough time. *Enough!*"

(Hope, Millennium)

Second coming 197

During his 1960 presidential campaign, John F. Kennedy often closed his speeches with the story of Colonel Davenport, the Speaker of the Connecticut House of Representatives.

One day in 1789, the sky of Hartford darkened ominously, and some of the representatives, glancing out the windows, feared the end was at hand.

Quelling a clamor for immediate adjournment, Davenport rose and said, "The Day of Judgment is either approaching or it is not. If it is not, there is no cause for adjournment. If it is, I choose to be found doing my duty. Therefore, I wish that candles be brought."

Rather than fearing what is to come, we are to be faithful till Christ returns. Instead of fearing the dark, we're to be lights as we watch and wait.

(Faithfulness, Service)

Security 198

During a hurricane in the Gulf of Mexico, a news report highlighted a rescue device used on the oil rigs. In case of fire or (in this case) hurricane, rig workers scramble into the bullet shaped "bus" and strap themselves into their seats. When the entry port is shut, the vehicle is released down a chute and projected away from the rig. The seat belts protect the occupants from the impact with the water. The capsule then bobs in the sea until the rescuers come to pick it up.

The device parallels the theological truth of Romans 8:1 —"Therefore, there is now no condemnation for those who are *in* Christ Jesus." Justification does not mean our world always stops falling apart. The rig still may topple in the hurricane. But those in the right place, whether a rescue module or spiritually in Christ, are saved from the ultimate consequences of the storm. The storm will take its course. The welfare of the workers depends on whether they are *in* the rescue device.

(Christ, Salvation)

Security 199

The 3-year-old felt secure in his father's arms as Dad stood in the middle of the pool. But Dad, for fun, began walking slowly toward the deep end, gently chanting, "Deeper and deeper and deeper," as the water rose higher and higher on the child. The lad's face registered increasing degrees of panic, and he held all the more tightly to his father, who, of course, easily touched the bottom.

Had the little boy been able to analyze his situation, he'd have realized there was no reason for increased anxiety. The water's depth in any part of the pool was over his head. Even in the shallowest part, had he not been held up, he'd have drowned. His safety anywhere in that pool depended on Dad.

At various points in our lives, all of us feel we're getting out of our depth—problems abound, a job is lost, someone dies. Our temptation is to panic, for we feel we've lost control. Yet, as with the child in the pool, the truth is we've never been in control over the most valuable things of life. We've always been held up by the grace of God, our Father, and that does not change. God is never out of his depth, and therefore we're as safe when we're "going deeper" as we have ever been.

(Trust, Father God)

Security 200

In a sermon, Juan Carlos Ortiz spoke of a conversation with a circus trapeze artist. The performer admitted the net underneath was there to keep them from breaking their necks, but added, "The net also keeps us from falling. Imagine there is no net. We would be so nervous that we would be more likely to miss and fall. If there wasn't a net, we would not dare to do some of the things we do. But because there's a net, we dare to make two turns, and once I made three turns—thanks to the net!"

Ortiz makes this observation: "We have security in God. When we are sure in his arms, we dare to attempt big things for God. We dare to be holy. We dare to be obedient. We dare, because we know the eternal arms of God will hold us if we fall."

(Faith, Obedience)

Seeking God 201

Columnist Herb Caen writes in the *San Francisco Chronicle*, "Every morning in Africa, a gazelle wakes up. It knows it must run faster than the fastest lion or it will be killed. Every morning a lion wakes up. It knows it must outrun the slowest gazelle or it will starve to death. It doesn't matter whether you are a lion or a gazelle; when the sun comes up, you'd better be running."

Spurgeon writes likewise, "If you are not seeking the Lord, the Devil is seeking you. If you are not seeking the Lord, judgment is at your heels."

In the Christian life, it's not enough simply to wake up. We are called to run, to become more like Christ, to press ahead in godliness.

(Godliness, Complacency)

Self-absorption 202

Clifton Fadiman, in *The Little, Brown Book of Anecdotes*, tells a story about Vladimir Nabokov, the Russian-born novelist who achieved popular success with his novels *Lolita* (1955), *Pale Fire* (1962), and *Ada* (1969).

One summer in the 1940s, Nabokov and his family stayed with James Laughlin at Alta, Utah, where Nabokov took the opportunity to enlarge his collection of butterflies and moths. Fadiman relates:

Nabakov's fiction has never been praised for its compassion; he was single-minded if nothing else. One evening at dusk he returned from his day's excursion saying that during hot pursuit near Bear Gulch he had heard someone groaning most piteously down by the stream.

"Did you stop?" Laughlin asked him.

"No, I had to get the butterfly."

The next day the corpse of an aged prospector was discovered in what has been renamed, in Nabokov's honor, Dead Man's Gulch.

While people around us are dying, how often we chase butterflies!

(Evangelism, Compassion)

Self-worth 203

At the Pan American Games, champion United States diver Greg Louganis was asked how he coped with the stress of international diving competition. He replied that he climbs to the board, takes a deep breath, and thinks, "Even if I blow this dive, my mother will still love me." Then he goes for excellence.

At the beginning of each day, how good it would be for each of us to take a deep breath, say, "Even if I blow it today, my God will still love me," and then, assured of grace, go into the day seeking a perfect 10!

(Mother, Love)

In Elmer Bendiner's book, *The Fall of Fortresses*, he describes one bombing run over the German city of Kassel:

Our B-17 (*The Tondelayo*) was barraged by flack from Nazi antiaircraft guns. That was not unusual, but on this particular occasion our gas tanks were hit. Later, as I reflected on the miracle of a twenty-millimeter shell piercing the fuel tank without touching off an explosion, our pilot, Bohn Fawkes, told me it was not quite that simple.

On the morning following the raid, Bohn had gone down to ask our crew chief for that shell as a souvenir of unbelievable luck. The crew chief told Bohn that not just one shell but eleven had been found in the gas tanks—eleven unexploded shells where only one was sufficient to blast us out of the sky. It was as if the sea had been parted for us. Even after thirty-five years, so awesome an event leaves me shaken, especially after I heard the rest of the story from Bohn.

He was told that the shells had been sent to the armorers to be defused. The armorers told him that Intelligence had picked them up. They could not say why at the time, but Bohn eventually sought out the answer.

Apparently when the armorers opened each of those shells, they found no explosive charge. They were as clean as a whistle and just as harmless. Empty? Not all of them.

One contained a carefully rolled piece of paper. On it was a scrawl in Czech. The Intelligence people scoured our base for a man who could read Czech. Eventually, they found one to decipher the note. It set us marveling. Translated, the note read: "This is all we can do for you now."

(Perseverance, Small things)

Servanthood 205

Bruce Thielemann, pastor of First Presbyterian Church in Pittsburgh, told of a conversation with an active layman, who mentioned, "You preachers talk a lot about giving, but when you get right down to it, it all comes down to basin theology."

Thielemann asked, "Basin theology? What's that?"

The layman replied, "Remember what Pilate did when he had the chance to acquit Jesus? He called for a basin and washed his hands of the whole thing. But Jesus, the night before his death, called for a basin and proceeded to wash the feet of the disciples. It all comes down to basin theology: Which one will you use?"

(Love, Duty)

Service 206

The folklore surrounding Poland's famous concert pianist and prime minister, Ignace Paderewski, includes this story:

A mother, wishing to encourage her young son's progress at the piano, bought tickets for a Paderewski performance. When the night arrived, they found their seats near the front of the concert hall and eyed the majestic Steinway waiting on stage.

Soon the mother found a friend to talk to, and the boy slipped away. When eight o'clock arrived, the spotlights came on, the audience quieted, and only then did they notice the boy up on the bench, innocently picking out "Twinkle, Twinkle, Little Star."

His mother gasped, but before she could retrieve her son, the master appeared on the stage and quickly moved to the keyboard.

"Don't quit—keep playing," he whispered to the boy. Leaning over, Paderewski reached down with his left hand and began filling in a bass part. Soon his right arm reached around the other side, encircling the child, to add a running obbligato. Together, the old master and the young novice held the crowd mesmerized.

In our lives, unpolished though we may be, it is the Master who surrounds us and whispers in our ear, time and again, "Don't quit—keep playing." And as we do, he augments and supplements until a work of amazing beauty is created.

(Weakness, Perseverance)

Don McCullough writes in *Waking from the American Dream*:

During World War II, England needed to increase its production of coal. Winston Churchill called together labor leaders to enlist their support. At the end of his presentation he asked them to picture in their minds a parade which he knew would be held in Piccadilly Circus after the war. First, he said, would come the sailors who had kept the vital sea lanes open. Then would come the soldiers who had come home from Dunkirk and then gone on to defeat Rommel in Africa. Then would come the pilots who had driven the Luftwaffe from the sky.

Last of all, he said, would come a long line of sweat-stained, soot-streaked men in miner's caps. Someone would cry from the crowd, "And where were you during the critical days of our struggle?"

And from ten thousand throats would come the answer, "We were deep in the earth with our faces to the coal."

Not all the jobs in a church are prominent and glamorous. But the people with their "faces to the coal" play a vital role in helping the church accomplish its mission.

(Humility, Body of Christ)

Service 208

Ted Engstrom in *The Pursuit of Excellence* writes:

I was cleaning out a desk drawer when I found a flashlight I hadn't used in over a year. I flipped the switch but wasn't surprised when it gave no light. I unscrewed it and shook it to get the batteries out, but they wouldn't budge.

Finally, after some effort, they came loose. What a mess! Battery acid had corroded the entire inside of the flashlight. The batteries were new when I'd put them in, and I'd stored them in a safe, warm place. But there was one problem. Those batteries weren't made to be warm and comfortable. The were designed to be turned on—to be used.

It's the same with us. We weren't created to be warm, safe, and comfortable. You and I were made to be "turned on"—to put our love to work, to apply our patience in difficult, trying situations—to let our light shine.

(Comforts, Security)

Sharing 209

In its January 25, 1988 issue, *Time* provided an insight on selfishness and its corollary, sharing. Speaking about the introduction of the videocassette recorder, the article said, "The company had made a crucial mistake. While at first Sony kept its Beta technology mostly to itself, JVC, the Japanese inventor of the VHS [format], shared its secret with a raft of other firms. As a result, the market was overwhelmed by the sheer volume of the VHS machines being produced."

This drastically undercut Sony's market share. The first year, Sony lost 40 percent of the market, and by 1987 it controlled only 10 percent. So now Sony has jumped on the VHS bandwagon. While it still continues to make Beta-format VHS's, Sony's switch to VHS, according to *Time,* will likely send Beta machines to "the consumer-electronics graveyard."

Even in a cut-throat business, sharing has its rewards.

(Selfishness, Greed)

Signs of the times 210

The May 1984 *National Geographic* showed through color photos and drawings the swift and terrible destruction that wiped out the Roman Cities of Pompeii and Herculaneum in 79 B.C.

The explosion of Mount Vesuvius was so sudden, the residents were killed while in their routine: men and women were at the market, the rich in their luxurious baths, slaves at toil. They died amid volcanic ash and superheated gasses. Even family pets suffered the same quick and final fate. It takes little imagination to picture the panic of that terrible day.

The saddest part is that these people did not have to die. Scientists confirm what ancient Roman writers record—weeks of rumblings and shakings preceded the actual explosion. Even an ominous plume of smoke was clearly visible from the mountain days before the eruption. If only they had been able to read and respond to Vesuvius's warning!

There are similar "rumblings" in our world: warfare, earthquakes, the nuclear threat, economic woes, breakdown of the family and moral standards. While not exactly new, these things do point to a coming day of Judgment (Matt. 24). People need not be caught unprepared. God warns and provides an escape to those who will heed the rumblings.

(Warnings, Judgment)

In 1982, "ABC Evening News" reported on an unusual work of modern art—a chair affixed to a shotgun. It was to be viewed by sitting in the chair and looking directly into the gunbarrel. The gun was loaded and set on a timer to fire at an undetermined moment within the next hundred years.

The amazing thing was that people waited in lines to sit and stare into the shell's path! They all knew that the gun could go off at point-blank range at any moment, but they were gambling that the fatal blast wouldn't happen during their minute in the chair.

Yes, it was foolhardy, yet many people who wouldn't dream of sitting in that chair live a lifetime gambling that they can get away with sin. Foolishly they ignore the risk until the inevitable self-destruction.

(Repentance, Complacency)

Sin 212

A man living in a forested area found his home overrun with mice—too many to exterminate with traps. So he bought a few boxes of D-Con and distributed them around the house, including one under his bed. That night he couldn't believe his ears; below him was a feeding frenzy.

In the morning he checked the box and found it licked clean.

Just to make sure the plan worked, he bought and placed another box. Again, the mice went for the flavored poison like piranha.

But the tasty and popular nighttime snack did its deadly work. In the days that followed, all was quiet. Just because something is popular doesn't mean it's good for you. In fact, it can be deadly—like sin.

(Popularity, World)

Time-lapse photography compresses a series of events into one picture. Such a photo appeared in an issue of *National Geographic*. Taken from a Rocky Mountain peak during a heavy thunderstorm, the picture captured the brilliant lightning display that had taken place throughout the storm's duration. The time-lapse technique created a fascinating, spaghetti-like web out of the individual bolts.

In such a way, our sin presents itself before the eyes of God. Where we see only isolated or individual acts, God sees the overall web of our sinning. What may seem insignificant —even sporadic—to us and passes with hardly a notice creates a much more dramatic display from God's panoramic viewpoint.

The psalmist was right when he wrote, "Who can discern his errors? Acquit me of hidden faults. Keep back your servant from presumptuous sins."

(Faults, Holiness)

Thomas Costain's history, *The Three Edwards*, describes the life of Raynald III, a fourteenth-century duke in what is now Belgium.

Grossly overweight, Raynald was commonly called by his Latin nickname, Crassus, which means "fat."

After a violent quarrel, Raynald's younger brother Edward led a successful revolt against him. Edward captured Raynald but did not kill him. Instead, he built a room around Raynald in the Nieuwkerk castle and promised him he could regain his title and property as soon as he was able to leave the room.

This would not have been difficult for most people since the room had several windows and a door of near-normal size, and none was locked or barred. The problem was Raynald's size. To regain his freedom, he needed to lose weight. But Edward knew his older brother, and each day he sent a variety of delicious foods. Instead of dieting his way out of prison, Raynald grew fatter.

When Duke Edward was accused of cruelty, he had a ready answer: "My brother is not a prisoner. He may leave when he so wills."

Raynald stayed in that room for ten years and wasn't released until after Edward died in battle. By then his health was so ruined he died within a year . . . a prisoner of his own appetite.

(Addiction, Appetites)

Mike Yaconelli writes in *The Wittenburg Door*:

I live in a small, rural community. There are lots of cattle ranches around here, and every once in a while a cow wanders off and gets lost. . . . Ask a rancher how a cow gets lost, and chances are he will reply, "Well, the cow starts nibbling on a tuft of green grass, and when it finishes, it looks ahead to the next tuft of green grass and starts nibbling on that one, and then it nibbles on a tuft of green grass right next to a hole in the fence. It then sees another tuft of green grass on the other side of the fence, so it nibbles on that one and then goes on to the next tuft. The next thing you know the cow has nibbled itself into being lost."

Americans are in the process of nibbling their way to lostness. . . . We keep moving from one tuft of activity to another, never noticing how far we have gone from home or how far away from the truth we have managed to end up.

(Backsliding, Lostness)

In *A View from the Zoo*, Gary Richmond, a former zoo keeper, has this to say:

Raccoons go through a glandular change at about 24 months. After that they often attack their owners. Since a 30-pound raccoon can be equal to a 100-pound dog in a scrap, I felt compelled to mention the change coming to a pet raccoon owned by a young friend of mine, Julie. She listened politely as I explained the coming danger.

I'll never forget her answer. "It will be different for me. . . ." And she smiled as she added, "Bandit wouldn't hurt me. He just wouldn't."

Three months later Julie underwent plastic surgery for facial lacerations sustained when her adult raccoon attacked her for no apparent reason. Bandit was released into the wild.

Sin, too, often comes dressed in an adorable guise, and as we play with it, how easy it is to say, "It will be different for me." The results are predictable.

(Warnings, Self-deception)

Sinful nature 217

"Pali, this bull has killed me." So said Jose Cubero, one of Spain's most brilliant matadors, before he lost consciousness and died.

Only 21 years old, he had been enjoying a spectacular career. However, in this 1985 bullfight, Jose made a tragic mistake. He thrust his sword a final time into a bleeding, delirious bull, which then collapsed. Considering the struggle finished, Jose turned to the crowd to acknowledge the applause.

The bull, however, was not dead. It rose and lunged at the unsuspecting matador, its horn piercing his back and puncturing his heart.

Just when we think them dead, sinful desires rise and pierce us from behind. We should never consider the sinful nature dead before we are.

(Temptation, Vigilance)

Sovereignty 218

In *Knowledge of the Holy,* A. W. Tozer attempts to reconcile the seemingly contradictory beliefs of God's sovereignty and man's free will:

An ocean liner leaves New York bound for Liverpool. Its destination has been determined by proper authorities. Nothing can change it. This is at least a faint picture of sovereignty.

On board the liner are scores of passengers. These are not in chains; neither are their activities determined for them by decree. They are completely free to move about as they will. They eat, sleep, play, lounge about on the deck, read, talk, altogether as they please; but all the while the great liner is carrying them steadily onward toward a predetermined port.

Both freedom and sovereignty are present here, and they do not contradict. So it is, I believe, with man's freedom and the sovereignty of God. The mighty liner of God's sovereign design keeps its steady course over the sea of history.

(Choices, Free will)

Sovereignty 219

During his days as guest lecturer at Calvin Seminary, R. B. Kuiper once used the following illustration of God's sovereignty and human responsibility:

I liken them to two ropes going through two holes in the ceiling and over a pulley above. If I wish to support myself by them, I must cling to them both. If I cling only to one and not the other, I go down.

I read the many teachings of the Bible regarding God's election, predestination, his chosen, and so on. I read also the many teachings regarding "whosoever will may come" and urging people to exercise their responsibility as human beings. These seeming contradictions cannot be reconciled by the puny human mind. With childlike faith, I cling to both ropes, fully confident that in eternity I will see that both strands of truth are, after all, of one piece.

(Free will, Responsibility)

Sowing and reaping 220

Several years after inventing radar, Sir Robert Watson Watt was arrested in Canada for speeding. He'd been caught in a radar trap. He wrote this poem:

Pity Sir Robert Watson Watt,
strange target of his radar plot,
and this, with others I could mention,
a victim of his own invention.

(Sin, Lawlessness)

Spiritual disciplines 221

National Geographic ran an article about the Alaskan bull moose. The males of the species battle for dominance during the fall breeding season, literally going head-to-head with antlers crunching together as they collide. Often the antlers, their only weapon, are broken, which ensures defeat.

The heftiest moose, with the largest and strongest antlers, triumphs. Therefore, the battle fought in the fall is really won during the summer, when the moose eat continually. The one that consumes the best diet for growing antlers and gaining weight will be the heavyweight in the fight. Those that eat inadequately sport weaker antlers and less bulk.

There is a lesson here for us. Spiritual battles await. Satan will choose a season to attack. Will we be victorious, or will we fall? Much depends on what we do now—before the wars begin. The bull-moose principle: Enduring faith, strength, and wisdom for trials are best developed before they're needed.

(Devotional life, Trials)

Spiritual disciplines 222

Awhile back on "The Merv Griffin Show," the guest was a body builder. During the interview, Merv asked, "Why do you develop those particular muscles?"

The body builder simply stepped forward and flexed a series of well-defined muscles from chest to calf. The audience applauded.

"What do you use all those muscles for?" Merv asked. Again, the muscular specimen flexed, and biceps and triceps sprouted to impressive proportions. "But what do you use those muscles for?" Merv persisted. The body builder was bewildered. He didn't have an answer other than to display his well-developed frame.

Our spiritual exercises—Bible study, prayer, reading Christian books, listening to Christian radio and tapes—are also for a purpose. They're meant to strengthen our ability to build God's kingdom, not simply to improve our pose before an admiring audience.

(Service, Devotional life)

A former park ranger at Yellowstone National Park tells the story of a ranger leading a group of hikers to a fire lookout. The ranger was so intent on telling the hikers about the flowers and animals that he considered the messages on his two-way radio distracting, so he switched it off. Nearing the tower, the ranger was met by a nearly breathless lookout, who asked why he hadn't responded to the messages on his radio. A grizzly bear had been seen stalking the group, and the authorities were trying to warn them of the danger.

Any time we tune out the messages God has sent us, we put at peril not only ourselves, but also those around us. How important it is that we never turn off God's saving communication!

(Prayer, Listening)

Spiritual perception 224

In his novel *My Lovely Enemy*, Canadian Mennonite Author Rudy Wiebe aptly pictures how different things look to the person with spiritual eyes:

It could be like standing on your head in order to see the world clearer. . . . If one morning you began walking on your hands, the whole world would be hanging. The trees, these ugly brick and tile buildings wouldn't be fixed here so solid and reassuring; they'd be pendant. The more safe and reliable they seem now, the more helpless they'd be then.

Once we are given "eyes to see," we recognize what a frail and temporary world we live in. We see the spiritual world as the solid one.

(World, Heaven)

Spiritual perception 225

Tim Hansel in *When I Relax I Feel Guilty* writes:

An American Indian was in downtown New York, walking with his friend who lived in New York City. Suddenly he said, "I hear a cricket."

"Oh, you're crazy," his friend replied.

"No, I hear a cricket. I do! I'm sure of it."

"It's the noon hour. There are people bustling around, cars honking, taxis squealing, noises from the city. I'm sure you can't hear it."

"I'm sure I do." He listened attentively and then walked to the corner, across the street, and looked all around. Finally on the corner he found a shrub in a large cement planter. He dug beneath the leaves and found a cricket. His friend was astounded. But the Cherokee said, "No. My ears are no different from yours. It simply depends on what you are listening to. Here, let me show you." He reached into his pocket and pulled out a handful of change—a few quarters, some dimes, nickels, and pennies. And he dropped it on the concrete. Every head within a block turned. "You see what I mean?" he said as he began picking up his coins. "It all depends on what you are listening for."

Not only must Christians have "ears to hear" (Matt. 13:9), but they must learn what to listen for.

(Money, Prayer)

Spiritual perception 226

A Coloradan moved to Texas and built a house with a large picture window from which he could view hundreds of miles of rangeland. "The only problem is," he said, "there's nothing to see."

About the same time, a Texan moved to Colorado and built a house with a large picture window overlooking the Rockies. "The only problem is I can't see anything," he said. "The mountains are in the way."

People have a way of missing what's right before them. They go to a city and see lights and glitter, but miss the lonely people. They hear a person's critical comments, but miss the cry for love and friendship.

(Sensitivity, Relationships)

Spiritual perception 227

A Denver woman told her pastor of a recent experience that she felt was a sign of the times. She'd walked into a jewelry store looking for a necklace. "I'd like a gold cross," she said.

The man behind the counter looked over the stock in the display case and said, "Do you want a plain one, or one with a little man on it?"

(Cross, Ignorance)

Spiritual perception 228

Roger von Oech in his book *A Kick in the Seat of the Pants*, suggests:

Take a look around where you're sitting and find five things that have blue in them. Go ahead and do it.

With a "blue" mindset, you'll find that blue jumps out at you: a blue book on the table, a blue pillow on the couch, blue in the painting on the wall, and so on. . . . In like fashion, you've probably noticed that after you buy a new car, you promptly see that make of car everywhere. That's because people find what they are looking for.

At times in our lives, God seems strangely absent, but the problem is not that God has disappeared. We simply lack a "God" mindset. When we develop our sensitivity, we soon begin to see his work everywhere.

(Faith, God's presence)

Spirituality 229

Our life in Christ can be compared to an aqueduct, the stone waterways that brought water from nearby mountains into parched cities in Italy and Spain, and that are still used in some countries today.

The objective foundation of our spiritual lives, the Word of God, is like the huge stone aqueduct itself. The subjective elements, our daily experience of Christ, is like the fresh water flowing through it.

Some Christians neglect the Word and seek only the subjective experience. But without the solid Word of God to contain and channel that experience, the experience itself drains away into error and is lost.

Other Christians boast well-engineered aqueducts based on extensive knowledge of the Bible, but they are bone dry. They bring no refreshment. Strong spiritual lives require both a strong knowledge of the Word of God and an intimate daily relationship with Christ.

(Scripture, Devotional life)

Stamina 230

A television documentary pointed out that the cheetah survives on the African plains by running down its prey. The big cat can sprint seventy miles per hour. But the cheetah cannot sustain that pace for long. Within its long, sleek body is a disproportionately small heart, which causes the cheetah to tire quickly. Unless the cheetah catches its prey in the first flurry, it must abandon the chase.

Sometimes Christians seem to have the cheetah's approach to ministry. We speed into projects with great energy. But lacking the heart for sustained effort, we fizzle before we finish. We vow to start faster and run harder, when what we need may be not more speed but more staying power—stamina that comes only from a bigger heart.

(Perseverance, Heart)

Stature 231

The growth chart had slipped from the playroom wall because the tape on its corners had become dry and brittle. Five-year-old Jordan hung it up again, meticulously working to get it straight. Then he stood his sister against the wall to measure her height.

"Mommy! Mommy! Anneke is forty inches tall!" he shouted as he burst into the kitchen. "I measured her."

His mom replied, "That's impossible, Sweetheart. She's only 3 years old. Let's go see." They walked back into the playroom, where the mother's suspicions were confirmed. Despite his efforts to hang the chart straight, Jordan had failed to set it at the proper height. It was several inches low.

We easily make Jordan's mistake in gauging our spiritual growth or importance. Compared to a shortened scale, we may appear better than we are. Only when we stand against the Cross, that "Great leveler of men" as A. T. Robertson called it, can we not think of ourselves "more highly than we ought to think." Christ, himself, must be our standard.

(Christlikeness, Pride)

Stewardship 232

According to a January 15, 1989 article in the *Lexington Herald-Leader*, the family living in a home in West Palm Beach, Florida, told a film crew it was okay to use the front lawn as a set for an episode of the "B.L. Stryker" television series. They knew cars would be crashing violently in front of the house.

While the front yard was being blown up, the owner of the home was tipped off and called from New York demanding to know what was happening to his house. It seems the people who were living in the house were only tenants and had no right to allow the property to be destroyed as the cameras rolled.

Many times we live our lives under the mistaken impression that they belong to us. Paul tells us we were "bought with a price." We must live as those who know God will call us to account for the ways we have used this life entrusted to us.

(Judgment, Lordship of Christ)

Jay Kesler writes in *Campus Life*:

There are two ways of handling pressure. One is illustrated by a bathysphere, the miniature submarine used to explore the ocean in places so deep that the water pressure would crush a conventional submarine like an aluminum can. Bathyspheres compensate with plate steel several inches thick, which keeps the water out but also makes them heavy and hard to maneuver. Inside they're cramped.

When these craft descend to the ocean floor, however, they find they're not alone. When their lights are turned on and you look through the tiny, thick plate-glass windows, what do you see? Fish!

These fish cope with extreme pressure in an entirely different way. They don't build thick skins: they remain supple and free. They compensate for the outside pressure through equal and opposite pressure inside themselves.

Christians, likewise, don't have to be hard and thick skinned—as long as they appropriate God's power within to equal the pressure without.

(Pressure, Power)

Submission 234

Stephen P. Beck writes:

Driving down a country road, I came to a very narrow bridge. In front of the bridge, a sign was posted: "Yield." Seeing no oncoming cars, I continued across the bridge and to my destination.

On my way back, I came to the same one-lane bridge, now from the other direction. To my surprise, I saw another "Yield" sign posted.

Curious, I thought. *I'm sure there was one positioned on the other side*.

When I reached the other side of the bridge, I looked back. Sure enough, yield signs had been placed at both ends of the bridge. Drivers from both directions were requested to give the other the right of way. It was a reasonable and gracious way of preventing a head-on collision.

When the Bible commands Christians to "be subject to one another" (Eph. 5:21), it is simply a reasonable and gracious command to let the other have the right of way and avoid interpersonal head-on collisions.

(Conflict, Meekness)

When Jewish psychiatrist Victor Frankl was arrested by the Nazis in World War II, he was stripped of everything—property, family, possessions. He had spent years researching and writing a book on the importance of finding meaning in life—concepts that later would be known as logotherapy. When he arrived in Auschwitz, the infamous death camp, even his manuscript, which he had hidden in the lining of his coat, was taken away.

"I had to undergo and overcome the loss of my spiritual child," Frankl writes. "Now it seemed as if nothing and no one would survive me; neither a physical nor a spiritual child of my own! I found myself confronted with the question of whether under such circumstances my life was ultimately void of any meaning."

He was still wrestling with that question a few days later when the Nazis forced the prisoners to give up their clothes.

"I had to surrender my clothes and in turn inherited the worn out rags of an inmate who had been sent to the gas chamber," says Frankl. "Instead of the many pages of my manuscript, I found in the pocket of the newly acquired coat a single page torn out of a Hebrew prayer book, which contained the main Jewish prayer, *Shema Yisrael* (Hear, O Israel! The Lord our God is one God. And you shall love the Lord your God with all your heart and with all your soul and with all your might.)

"How should I have interpreted such a 'coincidence' other than as a challenge to live my thoughts instead of merely putting them on paper?"

Later, as Frankl reflected on his ordeal, he wrote in his

book *Man's Search for Meaning*, "There is nothing in the world that would so effectively help one to survive even the worst conditions, as the knowledge that there is a meaning in one's life. . . . He who has a *why* to live for can bear almost any *how*."

(Meaning, Purpose)

Surrender 236

Bruce Larson, in *Believe and Belong*, tells how he helped people struggling to surrender their lives to Christ:

For many years I worked in New York City and counseled at my office any number of people who were wrestling with this yes-or-no decision. Often I would suggest they walk with me from my office down to the RCA Building on Fifth Avenue. In the entrance of that building is a gigantic statue of Atlas, a beautifully proportioned man who, with all his muscles straining, is holding the world upon his shoulders. There he is, the most powerfully built man in the world, and he can barely stand up under this burden. "Now that's one way to live," I would point out to my companion, "trying to carry the world on your shoulders. But now come across the street with me."

On the other side of Fifth Avenue is Saint Patrick's Cathedral, and there behind the high altar is a little shrine of the boy Jesus, perhaps eight or nine years old, and with no effort he is holding the world in one hand. My point was illustrated graphically.

We have a choice. We can carry the world on our shoulders, or we can say, "I give up, Lord; here's my life. I give you my world, the whole world."

(Burdens, Rest)

Time magazine carried the following news item:

When the post office in Troy, Michigan, summoned Michael Achorn to pick up a 2-foot-long, 40-pound package, his wife, Margaret, cheerfully went to accept it. But as she drove it back to her office in Detroit, she began to worry. The box was from Montgomery Ward, but the sender, Edward Achorn, was unknown to Margaret and her husband, despite the identical last name.

What if the thing was a bomb? She telephoned postal authorities. . . .

The bomb squad soon arrived with eight squad cars and an armored truck. They took the suspected bomb in the armored truck to a remote tip of Belle Isle in the middle of the Detroit River. There they wrapped detonating cord around the package and, as they say in the bomb business, "opened it remotely."

When the debris settled, all that was left intact was the factory warranty for the contents: a $450 stereo AM-FM receiver and a tape deck console. Now the only mystery is who is Edward Achorn and why did he send Michael and Margaret such a nice Christmas present?

Our suspicion ruins many of the finest gifts of life.

(Gifts, Skepticism)

Sympathy 238

When Edgar Guest, the American poet and writer, was a young man, his first child died. Writes Guest:

There came a tragic night when our first baby was taken from us. I was lonely and defeated. There didn't seem to be anything in life ahead of me that mattered very much.

I had to go to my neighbor's drugstore the next morning for something, and he motioned for me to step behind the counter with him. I followed him into his little office at the back of the store. He put both hands on my shoulders and said, "Eddie, I can't really express what I want to say, the sympathy I have in my heart for you. All I can say is that I'm sorry, and I want you to know that if you need anything at all, come to me. What is mine is yours."

[He was] just a neighbor across the way—a passing acquaintance. Jim Potter [the druggist] may long since have forgotten that moment when he gave me his hand and his sympathy, but I shall never forget it—never in all my life. To me it stands out like the silhouette of a lonely tree against a crimson sunset.

(Grief, Kindness)

Teaching 239

In 1947, a professor at the University of Chicago, Dr. Chandrasekhar, was scheduled to teach an advanced seminar in astrophysics. At the time he was living in Wisconsin, doing research at the Yerkes astronomical observatory. He planned to commute twice a week for the class, even though it would be held during the harsh winter months.

Registration for the seminar, however, fell far below expectations. Only two students signed up for the class. People expected Dr. Chandrasekhar to cancel, lest he waste his time. But for the sake of two students, he taught the class, commuting 100 miles round trip through back country roads in the dead of winter.

His students, Chen Ning Yang and Tsung-Dao Lee, did their homework. Ten years later, in 1957, they both won the Nobel prize for physics. So did Dr. Chandrasekhar in 1983.

For effective teachers, there is no such thing as a small class.

(Small things, Faithfulness)

A sea captain and his chief engineer were arguing over who was most important to the ship. To prove their point to each other, they decided to swap places. The chief engineer ascended to the bridge, and the captain went to the engine room.

Several hours later, the captain suddenly appeared on deck covered with oil and dirt. "Chief!" he yelled, waving aloft a monkey wrench. "You have to get down there: I can't make her go!"

"Of course you can't," replied the chief. "She's aground!"

On a team we don't excel each other; we depend on each other.

(Body of Christ, Service)

Temptation 241

Rick Green writes:

A former policeman with whom I stayed on a choir tour told me about being on duty during an ice storm. The ice was a half-inch thick on every tree in the area. He was called to a site where the ice and falling branches had caused a power line to come down; his duty was to keep people away from the area.

"There was a small tree near the fallen power line," he said, "the kind with a short trunk and lots of long thin branches. While that fallen power line was crackling and popping with electricity, it was throwing out sparks through the branches of that small tree. The sparks would reflect off the ice-covered branches sending out a rainbow of glimmering colors. I stood there and watched, and wondered how anything so beautiful could be so deadly."

I was reminded of the power of sin. We see something that seems beautiful, but when we reach out to touch, it becomes death to us.

(Sin, Deception)

Temptation 242

Portia Nelson has written a piece titled: *Autobiography in Five Short Chapters*. It reads:

Chapter 1—I walk down the street. There is a deep hole in the sidewalk. I fall in. I am lost. . . . I am helpless. It isn't my fault. It takes forever to find a way out.

Chapter 2—I walk down the same street. There is a deep hole in the sidewalk. I pretend I don't see it. I fall in again. I can't believe I am in the same place, but it isn't my fault. It still takes a long time to get out.

Chapter 3—I walk down the same street. There is a deep hole in the sidewalk. I see it is there. I still fall in. . . . It's a habit. My eyes are open. I know where I am. It is my fault. I get out immediately.

Chapter 4—I walk down the same street. There is a deep hole in the sidewalk. I walk around it.

Chapter 5—I walk down another street.

(Sin, Addiction)

Temptation 243

Reports the *Denver Post:*

Like many sheep ranchers in the West, Lexy Lowler has tried just about everything to stop crafty coyotes from killing her sheep. She has used odor sprays, electric fences, and "scare-coyotes." She has slept with her lambs during the summer and has placed battery-operated radios near them. She has corralled them at night, herded them at day. But the southern Montana rancher has lost scores of lambs—fifty last year alone.

Then she discovered the llama—the aggressive, funny-looking, afraid-of-nothing llama. . . . "Llamas don't appear to be afraid of anything," she said. "When they see something, they put their head up and walk straight toward it. That is aggressive behavior as far as the coyote is concerned, and they won't have anything to do with that. . . . Coyotes are opportunists, and llamas take that opportunity away."

Apparently llamas know the truth of what James writes: "Resist the Devil, and he will flee from you" (4:7). The moment we sense his attack is the moment we should face it and deal with it for what it is.

(Satan, Spiritual warfare)

Testimony 244

Dr. Paul Brand was speaking to a medical college in India on "Let your light so shine before men that they may behold your good works and glorify your Father." In front of the lectern was an oil lamp, with its cotton wick burning from the shallow dish of oil. As he preached, the lamp ran out of oil, the wick burned dry, and the smoke made him cough. He immediately used the opportunity.

"Some of us here are like this wick," he said. "We're trying to shine for the glory of God, but we stink. That's what happens when we use ourselves as the fuel of our witness rather than the Holy Spirit.

"Wicks can last indefinitely, burning brightly and without irritating smoke, if the fuel, the Holy Spirit, is in constant supply."

(Holy Spirit, Good works)

Testimony 245

On a wall near the main entrance to the Alamo in San Antonio, Texas, is a portrait with the following inscription:

James Butler Bonham—no picture of him exists. This portrait is of his nephew, Major James Bonham, deceased, who greatly resembled his uncle. It is placed here by the family that people may know the appearance of the man who died for freedom.

No literal portrait of Jesus exists either. But the likeness of the Son who makes us free can be seen in the lives of his true followers.

(Christlikeness, Witness)

Mark Tidd of Webster, New York, describes an experience from his college days:

An old man showed up at the back door of the house we were renting. Opening the door a few inches, we saw his eyes were glassy and his furrowed face glistened with silver stubble. He clutched a wicker basket holding a few unappealing vegetables. He bid us good morning and offered his produce for sale. We were uneasy enough that we made a quick purchase to alleviate both our pity and our fear.

To our chagrin, he returned the next week, introducing himself as Mr. Roth, the man who lived in the shack down the road. As our fears subsided, we got close enough to realize it wasn't alcohol but cataracts that marbleized his eyes. On subsequent visits, he would shuffle in, wearing two mismatched right shoes, and pull out a harmonica. With glazed eyes set on a future glory, he'd puff out old gospel tunes between conversations about vegetables and religion.

On one visit, he exclaimed, "The Lord is so good! I came out of my shack this morning and found a bag full of shoes and clothing on my porch."

"That's wonderful, Mr. Roth!" we said. "We're happy for you."

"You know what's even more wonderful?" he asked. "Just yesterday I met some people that could really use them."

(Giving, Generosity)

Thanksgiving 247

In a sermon at Immanuel Presbyterian Church in Los Angeles, Gary Wilburn said:

In 1636, amid the darkness of the Thirty Years' War, a German pastor, Martin Rinkart, is said to have buried five thousand of his parishioners in one year, an average of fifteen a day. His parish was ravaged by war, death, and economic disaster.

In the heart of that darkness, with the cries of fear outside his window, he sat down and wrote this table grace for his children:

Now thank we all our God
With heart and hands and voices;
Who wondrous things hath done,
In whom his world rejoices.
Who, from our mother's arms,
Hath led us on our way
With countless gifts of love
And still is ours today.

Here was a man who knew thanksgiving comes from love of God, not from outward circumstances.

(Contentment, Worship)

Traditions 248

William Poteet wrote in *The Pentecostal Minister* how in 1903 the Russian czar noticed a sentry posted for no apparent reason on the Kremlin grounds. Upon inquiry, he discovered that in 1776 Catherine the Great found there the first flower of spring. "Post a sentry here," she commanded, "so that no one tramples that flower under foot!"

Some traditions die hard.

(Change, Innovation)

M.C. Wesleyan 28Feb99

In *A View from the Zoo,* Gary Richmond tells about the birth of a giraffe:

The first thing to emerge are the baby giraffe's front hooves and head. A few minutes later the plucky newborn is hurled forth, falls ten feet, and lands on its back. Within seconds, he rolls to an upright position with his legs tucked under his body. From this position he considers the world for the first time and shakes off the last vestiges of the birthing fluid from his eyes and ears.

The mother giraffe lowers her head long enough to take a quick look. Then she positions herself directly over her calf. She waits for about a minute, and then she does the most unreasonable thing. She swings her long, pendulous leg outward and kicks her baby, so that it is sent sprawling head over heals.

When it doesn't get up, the violent process is repeated over and over again. The struggle to rise is momentous. As the baby calf grows tired, the mother kicks it again to stimulate its efforts. . . . Finally, the calf stands for the first time on its wobbly legs.

Then the mother giraffe does the most remarkable thing. She kicks it off its feet again. Why? She wants it to remember how it got up. In the wild, baby giraffes must be able to get up as quickly as possible to stay with the herd, where there is safety. Lions, hyenas, leopards, and wild hunting dogs all enjoy young giraffes, and they'd get it too, if the mother didn't teach her calf to get up quickly and get with it. . . .

I've thought about the birth of the giraffe many times. I can see its parallel in my own life. There have been many times when it seemed that I had just stood up after a trial, only to be knocked down again by the next. It was God helping me to remember how it was that I got up, urging me always to walk with him, in his shadow, under his care.

(Discipline, Pain)

A man found a cocoon of the emperor moth and took it home to watch it emerge. One day a small opening appeared, and for several hours the moth struggled but couldn't seem to force its body past a certain point.

Deciding something was wrong, the man took scissors and snipped the remaining bit of cocoon. The moth emerged easily, its body large and swollen, the wings small and shriveled.

He expected that in a few hours the wings would spread out in their natural beauty, but they did not. Instead of developing into a creature free to fly, the moth spent its life dragging around a swollen body and shriveled wings.

The constricting cocoon and the struggle necessary to pass through the tiny opening are God's way of forcing fluid from the body into the wings. The "merciful" snip was, in reality, cruel. Sometimes the struggle is exactly what we need.

(Struggles, Difficulties)

Trivialities 251

A familiar Mother Goose rhyme goes:

Pussy cat, Pussy cat, where have you been?
I've been to London to visit the queen.
Pussy cat, Pussy cat, what did you there?
I frightened a little mouse under the chair.

Like that cat, Christians sometimes settle for petty involvements, trivial pursuits—chasing mice—when we have the opportunity to spend time with royalty, with the King! Instead of remaining content with minimum daily requirements, we can deepen our relationship with God and grow into maturity.

(Maturity, Devotional life)

Trust 252

A television program preceding the 1988 Winter Olympics featured blind skiers being trained for slalom skiing, impossible as that sounds. Paired with sighted skiers, the blind skiers were taught on the flats how to make right and left turns.

When that was mastered, they were taken to the slalom slope, where their sighted partners skied beside them shouting, “Left!” and “Right!” As they obeyed the commands, they were able to negotiate the course and cross the finish line, depending solely on the sighted skiers’ word. It was either complete trust or catastrophe.

What a vivid picture of the Christian life! In this world, we are in reality blind about what course to take. We must rely solely on the Word of the only One who is truly sighted —God himself. His Word gives us the direction we need to finish the course.

(Direction, Scripture)

Truth 253

Sodium is an extremely active element found naturally only in combined form; it always links itself to another element. Chlorine, on the other hand, is the poisonous gas that gives bleach its offensive odor. When sodium and chlorine are combined, the result is sodium chloride—common table salt—the substance we use to preserve meat and bring out its flavor.

Love and truth can be like sodium and chlorine. Love without truth is flighty, sometimes blind, willing to combine with various doctrines. On the other hand, truth by itself can be offensive, sometimes even poisonous. Spoken without love, it can turn people away from the gospel.

When truth and love are combined in an individual or a church, however, then we have what Jesus called "the salt of the earth," and we're able to preserve and bring out the beauty of our faith.

(Love, Saltiness)

Unity 254

The May 1987 edition of *National Geographic* included a feature about the arctic wolf. Author L. David Mech described how a seven-member pack had targeted several musk-oxen calves who were guarded by eleven adults. As the wolves approached their quarry, the musk-oxen bunched in an impenetrable semicircle, their deadly rear hooves facing out, and the calves remained safe during a long standoff with the enemy.

But then a single ox broke rank, and the herd scattered into nervous little groups. A skirmish ensued, and the adults finally fled in panic, leaving the calves to the mercy of the predators. Not a single calf survived.

Paul warned the Ephesian elders in Acts 20 that after his departure wolves would come, not sparing the flock. Wolves continue to attack the church today but cannot penetrate and destroy when unity is maintained. When believers break ranks, however, they provide easy prey.

(Wolves, Satan)

Values 255

Helmut Thielicke in *How to Believe Again,* writes:

I once heard of a child who was raising a frightful cry because he had shoved his hand into the opening of a very expensive Chinese vase and then couldn't pull it out again. Parents and neighbors tugged with might and main on the child's arm, with the poor creature howling out loud all the while.

Finally there was nothing left to do but to break the beautiful, expensive vase. And then as the mournful heap of shards lay there, it became clear why the child had been so hopelessly stuck. His little fist grasped a paltry penny which he had spied in the bottom of the vase and which he, in his childish ignorance, would not let go.

(Money, Greed)

Norman Cousins, after his experiences at UCLA medical school, notes a common misunderstanding about what is "real" and "unreal."

In Bob Benson's *He Speaks Softly*, Cousins is quoted:

The words "hard" and "soft" are generally used by medical students to describe the contrasting nature of courses. Courses like biochemistry, physics, pharmacology, anatomy, and pathology are anointed with the benediction of "hard," whereas subjects like medical ethics, philosophy, history, and patient-physician relationships tend to labor under the far less auspicious label "soft". . . . [But] a decade or two after graduation there tends to be an inversion. That which was supposed to be hard turns out to be soft, and vice versa. The knowledge base of medicine is constantly changing. . . . But the soft subjects—especially those that have to do with intangibles—turn out in the end to be of enduring value.

(Ethics, Permanence)

J. Alistair Brown writes:

Walking through a park, I passed a massive oak tree. A vine had grown up along its trunk. The vine started small—nothing to bother about. But over the years the vine had gotten taller and taller. By the time I passed, the entire lower half of the tree was covered by the vine's creepers. The mass of tiny feelers was so thick that the tree looked as though it had innumerable birds' nests in it.

Now the tree was in danger. This huge, solid oak was quite literally being taken over; the life was being squeezed from it.

But the gardeners in that park had seen the danger. They had taken a saw and severed the trunk of the vine—one neat cut across the middle. The tangled mass of the vine's branches still clung to the oak, but the vine was now dead. That would gradually become plain as weeks passed and the creepers began to die and fall away from the tree.

How easy it is for sin, which begins so small and seemingly insignificant, to grow until it has a strangling grip on our lives.

But sin's power is severed by Christ, and gradually, as we yield daily to Christ, sin's grip dries up and falls away.

(Sin, Surrender)

Vigilance 258

Dean Niferatos was riding the Number 22 CTA bus in Chicago. The bus brimmed with dozing office workers, restless punkers, and affluent shoppers. At the Clark and Webster stop, two men and a woman climbed in. The driver, a seasoned veteran, immediately bellowed, "Everybody watch your valuables. There are pickpockets on board."

Women clutched their purses tightly. Men put their hands on their wallets. All eyes fixed on the trio, who, looking insulted and harassed, didn't break stride as they promptly exited through the middle doors.

The Bible warns us to be vigilant, because evil is less likely to overtake us when we're watching.

(Satan, Spiritual warfare)

Vigilance 259

Steve Green, who sang six years with Bill and Gloria Gaither, tells about getting to know some of the work crews in the large auditoriums where their concerts were held.

The Gaithers prefer concerts-in-the-round, which means extra work for the "riggers," who walk the four-inch rafter beams—often a hundred feet above the concrete floor—to hang sound speakers and spotlights. For such work, understandably, they are very well paid.

"The fellows I talked to weren't bothered by the sight of looking down a hundred feet," says Green. "What they *didn't* like, they said, were jobs in buildings that had false ceilings—acoustical tile slung just a couple of feet below the rafters. They were still high in the air, and if they slipped, their weight would smash right through the flimsy tile. But their minds seemed to play tricks on them, lulling them into carelessness."

Satan's business is not so much in scaring us to death as persuading us that the danger of a spiritual fall is minimal. No wonder Peter advised us to "resist him, standing firm in the faith" (1 Pet. 5:9).

(Deception, Temptation)

Vision 260

About 350 years ago a shipload of travelers landed on the northeast coast of America. The first year they established a town site. The next year they elected a town government. The third year the town government planned to build a road five miles westward into the wilderness.

In the fourth year the people tried to impeach their town government because they thought it was a waste of public funds to build a road five miles westward into a wilderness. Who needed to go there anyway?

Here were people who had the vision to see three thousand miles across an ocean and overcome great hardships to get there. But in just a few years they were not able to see even five miles out of town. They had lost their pioneering vision.

With a clear vision of what we can become in Christ, no ocean of difficulty is too great. Without it, we rarely move beyond our current boundaries.

(Change, Complacency)

Vision 261

In the book *A Saviour for All Seasons*, William Barker relates the story of a bishop from the East Coast who many years ago paid a visit to a small, midwestern religious college. He stayed at the home of the college president, who also served as professor of physics and chemistry. After dinner, the bishop declared that the millennium couldn't be far off, because just about everything about nature had been discovered and all inventions conceived.

The young college president politely disagreed and said he felt there would be many more discoveries. When the angered bishop challenged the president to name just one such invention, the president replied he was certain that within fifty years men would be able to fly.

"Nonsense!" sputtered the outraged bishop. "Only angels are intended to fly."

The bishop's name was Wright, and he had two boys at home who would prove to have greater vision than their father. Their names: Orville and Wilbur.

(Creativity, Skepticism)

When Apple Computer fell on difficult days a while back, Apple's young chairman, Steven Jobs, traveled from the Silicon Valley to New York City. His purpose was to convince Pepsico's John Sculley to move west and run his struggling company.

As the two men overlooked the Manhattan skyline from Sculley's penthouse office, the Pepsi executive started to decline Jobs's offer.

"Financially," Sculley said, "you'd have to give me a million-dollar salary, a million-dollar bonus, and a million-dollar severance."

Flabbergasted, Jobs gulped and agreed—if Sculley would move to California. But Sculley would commit only to being a consultant from New York. At that, Jobs issued a challenge to Sculley: "Do you want to spend the rest of your life selling sugared water, or do you want to change the world?"

In his autobiography *Odyssey*, Sculley admits Jobs's challenge "knocked the wind out of me." He said he'd become so caught up with his future at Pepsi, his pension, and whether his family could adapt to life in California that an opportunity to "change the world" nearly passed him by. Instead, he put his life in perspective and went to Apple.

Many people don't recognize a chance to change the world. Part of the Christian message is letting people know what a difference the gospel makes.

(Evangelism, Service)

Word of God 263

Any of us more than twenty-five years old can probably remember where we were when we first heard of President Kennedy's assassination in 1963.

British novelist David Lodge, in the introduction to one of his books, tells where he was—in a theater watching the performance of a satirical revue he had helped write. In one sketch, a character demonstrated his nonchalance in an interview by holding a transistor radio to his ear. The actor playing the part always tuned into a real broadcast.

Suddenly came the announcement that President Kennedy had been shot. The actor quickly switched it off, but it was too late. Reality had interrupted stage comedy.

For many believers, worship, prayer, and Scripture are a nonchalant charade. They don't expect anything significant to happen, but suddenly God's reality breaks through, and they're shocked.

(Reality, Church)

World 264

No one imagined that Charles Dutton would have achieved anything, for he spent many years imprisoned for manslaughter. But when someone asked this now-successful Broadway star of *The Piano Lesson* how he managed to make such a remarkable transition, he replied, "Unlike the other prisoners, I never decorated my cell."

Dutton had resolved never to regard his cell as home. Christians, too, accomplish much in this world when they don't accommodate themselves to it, but instead are "longing for a better country—a heavenly one" (Heb. 11:16).

(Heaven, Hope)

Worship 265

In *Touch and Live*, George Vandeman writes:

A young stranger to the Alps was making his first climb, accompanied by two stalwart guides. It was a steep, hazardous ascent. But he felt secure with one guide ahead and one following. For hours they climbed. And now, breathless, they reached for those rocks protruding through the snow above them—the summit.

The guide ahead wished to let the stranger have the first glorious view of heaven and earth, and moved aside to let him go first. Forgetting the gales that would blow across those summit rocks, the young man leaped to his feet. But the chief guide dragged him down. "On your knees, sir!" he shouted. "You are never safe here except on your knees."

(Reverence, Humility)

Index

All entries are referenced by illustration number not page number.